The Proceedings
of the
Seventh Annual Conference
of the
NAPOLEONIC SOCIETY OF AMERICA
October 11-13, 1991
Providence, Rhode Island

Published by

THE NAPOLEONIC SOCIETY OF AMERICA
1115 Ponce De Leon Boulevard
Clearwater, FL 34616
1-813-586-1779

Produced by
MouseTrap Design & Illustration
237 NW Royal Ct., Gresham, OR 97030

Copyright, 1992, The Napoleonic Society of America, Clearwater, FL
ISBN- 0-9631953-0-1

The Proceedings
of the
SEVENTH ANNUAL CONFERENCE
of the
NAPOLEONIC SOCIETY OF AMERICA
October 11- 13, 1991
Providence, Rhode Island

OFFICERS

Joseph M. Nicolazzo, Stratford, CT .... Treasurer
Robert M. Snibbe, Belleair, FL .... President & Managing Director
Ronald G. Tinlin, Richardson, TX .... Executive Vice President
Steven A. Williams, Huntingdon, TN .... Vice President
Robert D. Williams, Concord, MA .... Secretary

DIRECTORS

Class of 1991

Frederick W. G. Ackerman .... Sandusky, OH
J. Armand Gelinas, MD .... Largo, FL
Jacques Ouimette .... Montreal, QUE
Patricia Remler .... Riverdale, NY
Ellen L. Snibbe .... New York, NY

Class of 1992

Robin Bates .... Mesa, AZ
Robert Brier .... Riverdale, NY
Coburn Grabenhorst, Jr .... Salem, OR
Robert W. Marshall .... Lexington, KY
Col. Floyd W.McRae .... Atlanta, GA
Robert D. Williams .... Concord, MA

Class of 1993

Nicholas D. Ellis .... Belleair Beach, FL
John H. Fournier, MD .... Chicago, IL
Proctor Jones .... San Francisco, CA
Rev. James Parker .... Charleston, SC
Helen Smith .... Waterloo, ONT
Ronald G. Tinlin .... Richardson, TX

Class of 1994

Walter Etling .... Miami, FL
William Hurlbutt .... Lincolnshire, IL
Michael LaVean .... Saranac, MI
Joseph M. Nicolazzo .... Stratford, CT
Timothy Pickles .... New Orleans, LA
Lawrence Polyak .... Rochester Hills, MI

THE NAPOLEONIC SOCIETY OF AMERICA

The Napoleonic Society of America is a non-profit membership organization that was founded to provide people interested in the Napoleonic era with a means of communicating with and sharing views with thousands of others who are also interested in Napoleon as a man, as a military genius, as an extraordinary administrator, and as a legend.

Over 1,350 members have joined from the United States, Canada, and in 23 foreign countries. They receive a handsome membership pin, a membership card, and the 40-page MEMBER'S BULLETIN regularly.

The BULLETIN covers a wide variety of topics such as social and political history, medicine, art and military sciences. It also reviews the latest literature, memoirs, letters and other data which are constantly being uncovered, as well as upcoming activities and events both in the USA and abroad.

The BULLETIN also reports on visits to Napoleonic sites, battlefields and museums, includes notices of exhibits, auctions and re-enactments, items for sale and wanted, book reviews, letters-to-the-editor, and sources of books, prints, miniatures, medals, stamps, coins, weapons and militaria, wargaming, re-enactments and much more. The Society also organizes Annual Conferences which give members the opportunity to hear excellent talks by noted historians or by fellow members who are experts in their own areas of special interest. At these conferences, which last three days, dealers in Napoleonic memorabilia are encouraged to display their items at a *Marché des Antiquaires,* the largest collection of Napoleonic artifacts for sale in the United States.

Finally, members are able to join Annual Tours organized by the Society to visit the most important Napoleonic sites in France and Europe. Members stay in first class hotels, travel in air conditioned buses, and everywhere they go they are accompanied by English speaking scholars or curators who take them behind the scenes to see things normally seen only by VIPs or scholars.

Copies of a sample MEMBER'S BULLETIN and a Membership Application are available free on request.

The Napoleonic Society of America
1115 Ponce de Leon Blvd. Clearwater FL 34616
A Non-profit Membership Corporation, founded in 1983
Telephone- Days- 813-586-1779 • Evenings or weekends- 813-584-1255

CONTENTS

Toast to the Emperor 1
   by Father James Parker
A New Book About Napoleon 2
   by Proctor Jones
Weapons of Honor and The Legion of Honor 7
   by Coburn Grabenhorst, Jr.
Costume During the Napoleonic Wars 17
   by Timothy Pickles
Napoleon's Administrative "Army" –His Prefects 23
   by Robert D. Williams
Napoleon - The Name and the Saint 39
   by Frank Dello Stritto
Napoleon - An Operational Genius But a Strategic Failure 56
   by Professor Steven Ross
Francs, Family and Frontiers 70
   by Timothy Kirkpatrick
The Three Napoleonic Collections at Brown University 76
   by Peter Harrington
Napoleonic Nobility and Its Offshoots 79
   by Derwin Mak
In "Defense" of Napoleon–Napoleon's Domestic Legacy 87
   by J. David Markham
Borodino: 1812 and 180 Years Later, 1992 99
   by Major Wilbur E. Gray

Round Table Discussions
Theme-"Napoleon and His Sponsorships of the Arts"

Napoleon's Cultivation of the Arts–Sculpture 111
   by James Jahnke
French Porcelain 117
   by Helen Smith
Egyptology 126
   by Arthur Lawson
Uniforms in the Age of Napoleon 129
   by William B. Teefy
Goldsmiths and Silversmiths 132
   by Robert W. Marshall

Toast To The Emperor

As a lawgiver, he is rivaled by few in the annals of jurisprudence. He presided personally over much of the work on the Code with takes his name.

As a leader of men, he was renowned. His personal mystique and the love his troops manifested were strong contributions to the might and the mystery of the Grande Armée.

As a general and a tactician he was without peer in all history. He made decisions beyond the abilities of the great captains of battle.

As master of the French nation, he was concerned not only for his own posterity, but also for the glory of France. And he gave that glory to the French people.

As Consul and Sovereign he encouraged education, restored the Church to France, inspired the spirit of the people, freed slaves, gave the freedom of law to conquered lands, shed his own glory on the army, and had greater influence on everything in his time than anyone before or after him.

Ladies and Gentlemen,…to His Imperial Majesty, the Emperor of the French!

Vive l'Empereur!

–By Father James Parker
Charleston, SC

A New Book on Napoleon
By Proctor Jones, San Francisco, CA

I am one of some 250,000 persons who has chosen to publish a book about Napoleon Bonaparte and his era. When you think of all of the people who have existed in the world since 1821, you see that I am one of a rather select class. However of all the 250,000 other writers, I am, I believe, the only one who has sought to edit Napoleon's story as lived by two men who were so intimately attached to his every-day life — his valet and his secretary.

Through our organization I met Charles-Otto Zieseniss, Secretary-General of the *Le Souvenir Napoléonien* in Paris, whom many of you know. He became my friend and adviser. Through him I met most of the other members of the present Napoleonic family. I met Count Alexandre Walewski and his lovely wife. When both became aware of my intention to produce this book, they permitted me to use materials from a dictation of the Comtesse Marie Walewska relating the details of how she met Napoleon.

Through one of our members, John Morse, I was led to the tomb of the Comtesse in the *Pere Lachaise* cemetery. At first I thought the tomb held a death mask of this remarkable lady, but inquiry of the d'Ornano family disclosed that what was there was the death mask of the Marshal d'Ornano. You may look into the tomb today. The mask is on the left along with a plaster cast of the Marshal's hand. However, in the center of the vault is an urn which contains the heart of Marie Walewska. She had married a distant relative of Napoleon following his exile to St. Helena.

Winston Churchill described his experience in writing a book, saying that he approached his work like a lover his mistress, enamoured of his subject, warmed by the heat of nascent discovery. Eventually as the work took shape, he viewed it more as a connubial duty; eventually as a duty enforced in wifely fashion to which he was at various times disinclined. Then the book took the form of a carping critic, finally became his mother-in-law; and the last miserable moments of putting together the index, an ungrateful child. Once in print, however, with his name neatly shown on the cover, it engendered love rekindled.

I must admit there were times when I wondered if I could adequately tame the material I had at hand. I would awaken in the dark of night in a cold sweat, filled with concern about what you and other Napoleonic experts would think of me and of this work. I saw myself as an interloper creeping stealthily into your private domain, invading your Napoleon.

I also was concerned from a psychiatric point of view, not so much by the fact that I was paying so much attention to Napoleon that I occasionally tried on his hat to see if it fit, but that I played a great deal with scissors. This of course has been a cut and paste job because I had to re-edit some 2,000 pages from three volumes each of Meneval and Constant. The only saving grace was that although I felt like it, I did not get to the point of cutting out paper dolls. I must have gone through 9,000 pieces of paper. Anyway, I finally completed the paste-up and then I had to descend into the cauldron of choosing photographs, writing captions, being sure that the captions were right, and being sure that the pictures were right. We used the photographic library services in Paris and the National Museums.

It was all a very expensive process, and when I finish paying for the world rights for all that I have used, the tab will probably be something like $40,000. But I think the book will be of solid interest even to people who know nothing about Napoleon. And to this extent, certainly, this effort has been worthwhile.

I am encouraged by the fact that Random House has seen fit to pick the book up for distribution and foreign editions. The work will present over 300 color reproductions, mostly from the important collections of Napoleonic paintings. Many of them will help the imagination to take you back to Napoleonic times. There will be a schedule of prices for various editions, ranging from $95 to $180 for the Premier Edition. I am presently working on these details with Random House.

The fact that Otto Zieseniss stayed with me, giving me quiet suggestions and encouragement kept me together.

He also introduced me to Professor Jean Tulard of the Sorbonne, whom, as you may know, is one of the leading Napoleonic editors in France and a recognized scholar. This gentleman has seen fit to write the introduction to the book, and as he saw most of it before he agreed to do so, I am encouraged by his support. Well, the job is done for better or for worse.

Obviously, the years spent with the Secretary and the Valet have led me to various conclusions relative to Napoleon, and these I will try to share with you.

First of all, it is astonishing to me that such very young men, Napoleon included, could take over the sovereign operation of a country as badly torn to pieces as France was — and succeed in making something of it.

2. I can accept the efforts of Napoleon and his associates to steady the government by establishing certain powers such as the First Consul for ten years, and then the First Consul for life. Even the establishment of the Empire. I think these efforts, which might appear self-serving, helped the country hold itself together in the face of England and other European predators.

3. I marvel at the speed with which Napoleon got around. Doing those trips in an automobile would take it out of a normal man — but by carriage. It is almost unbelievable.

4. His complete hands-on leadership in every corner of the government is another eye-opener. How could he operate so completely even when he was absent from Paris for such long periods of time?

5. Clear and far-seeing in most of his appointments, how could he have suffered men like Fouché, Talleyrand, and Bernadotte? All obvious troublemakers whose disloyalty was constantly apparent to him.

6. I cannot understand how in the last moments he was able to hold himself together when everything and everybody fell away from him. I did not know before of his effort to commit suicide.

7. Comtesse Walewska, I believe, was his best friend and somehow seemed to understand him perfectly. He should have taken advantage of her noble background and married her.

8. His advance on Moscow should have been for the same purpose that Jimmy Doolittle led the raid on Tokyo, namely to show Alexander that he could get there. He should have hit his target and departed.

9. Napoleon frightened the English with his remarks about eastern trade. This, with his success knocking about the customers of the Rothschilds in the Germanies discouraged any real chance of a rapprochment with England. England was borrowing the Rothschild's German profits.

10. As Napoleon rose, those around him took on greater honors which in turn reflected on Napoleon to the point where I think he felt a false sense of security and lost sight of his own vulnerability.   11. I believe Napoleon after the Peace of Amiens should have fortified his own borders as they existed in 1800, and from his strong trading position, make economic treaties which would would have benefitted not only France but could have led to the unification of Europe based on the sagging foundations of the old Hanseatic system.

12. Napoleon on Elba should have really established the universal collegiate of scholars about which he spoke.

My next work as far as Napoleon is concerned will involve his captivity on Elba, Waterloo, and eventually St. Helena. That work will not be so involved as the years of supremacy and will probably be a cut-and-paste job too. However, this time I'm going to get sharper scissors.

Now my job on the years of supremacy is done. I can only hope that it will be accepted by you for what it is.

* * *

Proctor Jones was born in 1916 in Cleveland, Ohio. His grandmother, a descendent of the French settlers of Detroit who arrived with

Cadillac in 1701, insisted that he be given French lessons at an early age, and thus began his live-long fascination with French history.

The culmination of this fascination is Napoleon, An Intimate Account of the Years of Supremacy, 1800 to 1814. *Mr. Jones spared no effort in assembling and editing this extraordinary, sumptuous volume.*

He is also the author of four novels, two photographic books on contemporary Russia, and Idylls of France, *which combines his own photographs with the writings of 18th- and 19th century English and American travelers. He is the owner of a publishing company, Honorary Consul General of Tunisia, a professional photographer, and a lawyer. He was educated at Case Western Reserve University, Stanford, and Harvard, and served in the Army during World War II. Mr. Jones is married and has six children, eight grandchildren, and two great-grandchildren. He lives in San Francisco.*

Weapons of Honor and the Legion of Honor

by Coburn L. Grabenhorst, Jr., Salem, OR

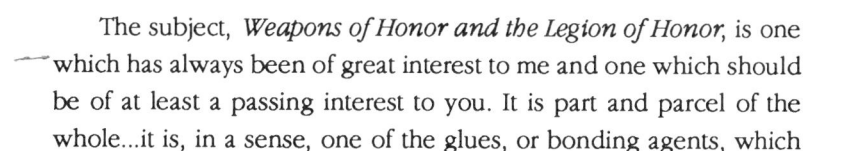

The subject, *Weapons of Honor and the Legion of Honor*, is one which has always been of great interest to me and one which should be of at least a passing interest to you. It is part and parcel of the whole...it is, in a sense, one of the glues, or bonding agents, which inspired achievement and accomplishment in the First Empire.

I share with you several quotes, perhaps accurate, perhaps merely paraphrases of the originals which Napoleon has been given authorship.

It is with baubles that men are led.

Men are led by toys.

Frenchmen love greatness and admire even the semblance of it.

A soldier will fight long and hard for a bit of metal and a piece of cloth.

Give me enough medals for my soldiers and I will conquer the world.

Although these few remarks may appear to be somewhat cynical, I believe they exemplify Napoleon's awareness of the psychological effect an awards or honors system would have. Signs of distinction did, indeed, become very important to the Frenchman. They were eagerly sought and highly prized, both military and civilian. Their value never diminished. And, aside from those given the Marshals and some of the generals and top civilian administrators, the same awards were given regardless of rank or station in life. The honor they represented was one and the same for each recipient...and, for all recipients. They were, thus and for the most part, all inclusive.

Now, we must realize, and I'm sure you do, that the honors given in these times excluded women, unless she was by birth or marriage a queen or princess. There were exceptions, however, but they were so very few.

I feel it important to express here that with the Revolution, the radical and liberal elements as we would refer to them today, wanted to do away with all outward expressions of distinction. And, on 30 July 1791, the Constitutional Convention, by decree, did just that with one very significant but short-lived exception. The Convention retained the **Order of St. Louis** originally instituted in 1693 by Louis XIV, renaming it the **Military Order**. There was still the feeling that valor had to be honored as France, the upstart Republic amongst countries ruled by royal houses, still had enemies and subsequent battles to fight. But 17 October 1792 saw this last decoration abolished also. If there is any other reason that the **Order of St. Louis** survived at all, then it was probably because the Order had been created to reward military merit *regardless* of the social class of one's birth. Its ultimate failure may well be due to the fact that the *only* military personnel who could receive it were army and navy *officers*, who if not already nobility were certainly in an upper class position due to their rank. Also, Protestants were not eligible to receive it.

However, a year or so later, an award of honor was promoted by Representative MarieJoseph Chenier at the National Convention for the heroic actions of one Lieutenant Breteche who saved his General from being captured at the Battle of Jemappes on 6 November 1792. Lt. Breteche survived a total of forty-one sword wounds to receive the first Sword of Honor given by the Convention.

More arms of honor were awarded over the next several years. However, development of the program became more noticeable during the Directory and Consulate periods.

In April 1797, Bonaparte, on campaign in Italy, ignited the institution of weapons of honor, more correctly called *Armes de Recompense*. He directed Berthier, his Chief of Staff, to have 100 sabres of grenadier and cavalry grade made with damascus blades and doree handles. Damascus blades are made from sheets of iron, or iron and steel, that are forged into one sheet of thinner dimension under great pressure, then cut and shaped. Doree is a process of gilding with gold something made of a less valuable metal alloy such as brass or bronze, the appearance being that it is made of gold. Furthermore, the name of the division and brigade would be placed in gold on one side of the blade, and on the other side of the blade, also in gold, would be "Given by the French Republic, General Bonaparte, *(name of citizen and – Year of the Republic.")*

Work was completed on these swords in November 1797 but the subsequent distribution was halted on the eve of the expedition to Egypt. There were thirty-eight swords awarded to the Massena division, three to the Bernadotte division, seven to the Serurier division, eighteen to the Joubert division, five to the Delmas division, seven to the Victor division, and two to the cavalry division. The two drummer boys who had led the assault on the bridge at Arcole received silver drumsticks. Not all were awarded. In March 1800, Napoleon having become First Consul, ordered the remainder to be made at Versailles.

These 100 sabres of the Army of Italy were the foundation of the *Armes de Recompense* of the Consulate. Interestingly, only three are known to exist. They are in the Museum of the Army, the Legion of Honor Museum, and in a private collection.

The date 7 November 1797 is an important date in this process because it was decreed on this date that all such arms would be made at Versailles under the direction of Nicholas Noel Boutet.

In 1799 the Minister of War ordered 400 sabres made for actions in the Egyptian campaign. They are known as the "sabres of the 400 brave," and are extremely hard to find.

When we say "arms of honor," it is not always an arm or weapon. Trumpets, drumsticks or batons, and small hatchets or boarding axes for navy personnel were a few of the nonweapons given for heroic action. Even though some sources differ as to the total number of *armes de recompense* awarded, the figure 2,104 seems reasonable, and breaks down as follows:

Sabres 655	Batons 47
Muskets 851	Trumpets 16
Carbines 247	Hatchets 50
Grenades 219	Pistols, etc. 19

Actions involving the capture of a flag, cannon or high-ranking officer could often merit the award of an arm of honor. In addition to the award, each recipient was granted an increase in pay of one cent per day, and *special* swords of honor recipients received double pay.

Boutet, the artist-director of arms manufacturing at Versailles had an exclusive contract with the French government to produce muskets, carbines, pistols, and sabres of honor. The muskets and carbines were inspired by the (flintlock) system 1777, all furniture (metal parts other than barrel and ramrod) were made of silver. A shield-like plaque adorned the stock. There were two types used, one merely signifying the award, the other giving a more detailed presentation.

The sabres were of three types, signifying light cavalry, heavy cavalry and infantry officers. A briquet (shorter infantry sword) was given to soldiers and NCO's. The blades were manufactured at Klingenthal. The richness of these sabres is the handles and scabbard bracelets, made of silver.

These weapons made at Versailles were beautiful...elegant awards of honor. They were made for both parade and battle. They were extremely personal and descended in the family. If, however, a family became destitute, the Minister of War would purchase them back for the State. Today, most are in the Museum of the Army, and a few are in private collections. It is estimated that perhaps only 250 are in existence.

The grenades and hatchets were plaques made for wear, while trumpets and drumsticks were made for use. I think we can safely say that these are extremely rare also.

The *Armes de Recompense* program was with few exceptions replaced by the institution of a new orders and decorations system in 1804, coinciding closely with Napoleon's coronation as Emperor and the creation of the Marshalate. The first and most important order created was the Order of the Legion of Honor. And it is this order that comprises the second half of this address.

The idea of an honors institution was first mentioned by Napoleon following a dinner at Malmaison with a group of advisors and state councilors. It was to be both civil and military and for both merit and bravery and for all members of society, not just the rich and/or elite. This was probably in April 1802. A few days later Napoleon met with his two secretaries, Meneval and Bourrienne, and drew up the project.

On 4 May 1802 Roederer presented this project to the Council of State, saying, "The Legion of Honor is a moral institution which will add strength to that most powerful of French motives, Honor." It took four sittings to bring it to a vote, finally passing 56 to 38. Later it was passed 166 to 110 by the Legislative Assembly.

By decree, the Legion of Honor was established on 19 May 1802. It was to be a personal recompense, non-transferable and carrying no title. It was the beginning of a new State attitude and policy towards rewarding meritable actions and services. The 2,104 soldiers recompensed with arms of honor earlier were the first to be mentioned to membership in this new institution.

The design of the medal was to be a star, with five double-pointed rays of white enamel, with a center medallion comprising the profile head of Napoleon encircled with the legend "*NAPOLEON EMP. DES FRANCAIS*" in blue enamel, inside a crown of oak and laurel leaves enameled green running between the white rays of the star. The central medallion on the reverse would be the Imperial Eagle inside the legend "*HONNEUR ET PATRIE*" enameled in blue. It would be suspended from a ribbon of red moire silk or satin, quite similar in color to the ribbon of the Order of St. Louis. All center medallions were to be made of gold except for the Legionnaire grade which would be of silver.

Originally there were to be four grades, or classes, of the Order, each class limited to membership and each carrying with it a yearly stipend. The grades, the number of members per grade, and stipend for each member was as follows:

> Grand Officers–105 members 5000 francs each
> Commander– 300 members 2000 francs each
> Officers– 450 members 1000 francs each
> Legionnaires– 3750 members 250 francs each

The Order was administered by a Grand Council of seven members, and divided into sixteen cohorts quartered in former palaces or abbeys with extensive properties to manage. The monies raised from the business endeavors of the cohorts was to pay the cost of the annual stipends to Legionnaires and fund other projects of the Order. However, the Legion grew in membership at a greater rate than the cohorts could support, so little by little the State played a greater role in funding the National Order.

The initial Grand Council was comprised of Napoleon, Cambaceres, Lebrun, Joseph Bonaparte, Lucien Bonaparte, General Kellerman, and Senator Lacepede. The cohorts were administered under the auspices of Berthier, Mortier, Bessieres, Soult, Lefebvre, Davout, Ney, Bernadotte, Lannes, Decres, Moncey, Murat, Bruix, Massena, Augereau and Jourdan.

The day following Napoleon's elevation as Emperor on 18 July 1804, he instituted the Legion of Honor and created the Marshalate. Within two months, on the fifteenth anniversary of the taking of the Bastille, 15 July 1804, the first distribution of the medals, or crosses, of the Legion of Honor was made near *Les Invalides*. The second distribution of crosses was made on 16 August 1804 at the Boulogne Camp where Napoleon was assembling the army with which he intended to invade England. The initial list of some 6000 recipients did include the 18 marshals, all the generals, colonels, and high-ranking naval officers, and most of the bishops and great men of the day. At both investitures and after personally receiving his decoration from the Emperor, all recipients in unison swore allegiance to him. There were few who declined to do so. Of those who balked at taking the oath were two Frenchmen who helped us, America, gain our freedom from King George III, namely La Fayette and Rochambeau.

Over the next eighteen months, several interesting and significant changes developed. The month following the investiture of the first Legionnaires, the Grand Council of the Order voted to admit into its ranks distinguished foreigners. And, in January, 1805, a fifth and highest grade of the Order was created. To be known as the "Grand Eagle", it could not exceed 60 in membership, exclusive of the Imperial Family, and monarchs and dignitaries of foreign states. Awards to foreigners, regardless of the grade of award, carried no stipend.

The insignia of the Grand Eagle class of the Order would be comprised of a wide moire silk or satin sash worn from right shoulder to left hip, the badge of the Order suspended therefrom. In addition, a large breast star embroidered in silver bullion and/or silver sequins, containing five double-pointed rays with a central Imperial Eagle, the eagle encircled by the legend "*HONNEUR ET PATRIE*" would be worn on the left breast.

Two weeks after Austerlitz, on 15 December 1805, the Grand Council voted to create five schools to provide free education to daughters of Legionnaires killed in action. Queen Hortense, Josephine's daughter and former pupil of Madame Campan, became its patron. And, Madam Campan became the director of the first of these schools. Only three were ever operational, opening respectively in 1806 (300 students), 1809 (300 students) and

1811 (200 students). Subsequently, daughters of living Legionnaires were admitted, and eventually some 20% of the enrollment were paying students.

Now, this is extraordinarily important as it was the first time in modern history that common women were given direct benefits from their father's military service. Also, it is extremely significant because it was a vehicle enabling women to better their position in life through a state-sponsored educational program. And, because it was directed by the ladies of the First Empire's government and social elite, the students learned certain skills and graces that could guide their future lives and perhaps enhance their opportunities.

In February 1808 the Legion abolished the cohorts system which it had originally established to finance its awards and activities, turning its properties over to the State. From this time on the State would pay recompenses to Legionnaires and fund the schools for Legionnaire's daughters and other programs of the Legion. And in so doing the State reconfirmed its belief in the organization, its purpose, and its endeavors.

The following month, the Emperor issued a decree restoring the concept and practice of creating titles of nobility, and confirming on Legionnaires the grades of Knight or Chevalier. This carried with it the recipient's right to a coat-of-arms.

On 3 March 1810, a decree was issued declaring the title of Chevalier transferable upon death to the eldest son. The proper patents for this transfer had to be approved by the Grand Chancellor of the Order.

Four years later, on 4 June 1814, Louis XVIII confirmed the continuance of the Order of the Legion of Honor, but changed part of the detailing of the decoration. Napoleon, returning from Elba, reversed and annulled these changes, only to have them reversed again after his defeat at Waterloo and Louis' subsequent return.

The Legion, at least 37,000 members strong, was indeed a formidable institution.

Comprising men of arms, civilian administrators, clergy and normal citizens, the Legion of Honor was truly people-oriented. In his wisdom, Louis saw the need to retain it... it was logical, practical, and sensible. Particularly in view of the fact that the King eagerly sought the experienced professional and wanted and needed the support of the civilian members from all walks of life.

Interestingly, Louis XVIII officially approved the hereditary passing of this Order in 1814; however, less than 1000 citizens took advantage of this rare privilege. He also canceled the annual stipend to civilian members retaining it only for awards of a military nature. And even though he re-instituted the Order of St. Louis and several other royal orders, the Legion of Honor was proudly honored and sought.

I would like to mention that there were three changes to the design of the medal or decoration of the Order during the First Empire. They are referred to as "types" by medalists and numismatists. Type I (1802 - 1806), the original mentioned above, was suspended from its ribbon merely by a suspension ring passing through a ball at the top arm of the cross. Type II (1806 - 1808), was different by the addition of a crown attached solidly to the two tips of the top arm (ray) and the ball through which the suspension ring passed, the ball surmounted by a small cross. Type III (1808 - 1812), differs from the others because the crown was attached to the top arm with a movable joint. Type IV (1812 - 1814, 1815), differed yet again by the addition of small balls on each of the tips of the five arms, some ten in all.

In conclusion, I would like to say that Napoleon did, so to speak, create a new aristocracy open to French citizens who by their valor, endeavors, talents and/or dedication brought credit and acclaim to France and her new method of State and Civil organization. The Order of the Legion of Honor with its five grades became the pattern for numerous other national orders and the prototype of the modern honors system. (Even the Legion of Merit in our own country is based on this system, the only one of America's decorations awarded in more than one class, the upper three grades reserved for foreigners.) The recipients of the Order were Napoleon's companions in arms and partners in civil service...they were the insurers of the French future. He succeeded to a very great degree. His successors have retained the Legion of Honor to this day.

Bibliography
- Administration des Monnaies et Medailles. *Decorations Officielles Francaises,* Imprimerie Nationale, Paris, 1956
- Adolphe, Daniel. Various notes and thoughts on the subject of *Armes de Recompense*
- Bottet, Capitaine Maurice. *Nicolas Boutet et la Manufacture de Versailles,* Jacques Grancher, Editeur, Paris, 1984 (?)
- Bottet, Maurice. *Monographies de l'Armee Blanche 1789-1870,* Aux Editions Haussmann, Paris, 1959
- Bourdier, C. *Les Ordres Francais et les Recompenses Nationales,* 2eme edition, L'Imprimerie Aubert S. A., Versailles, France, 1977

- Chandler, David G. *Dictionary of Napoleonic Wars*, Macmillan Publishing Co., Inc., New York, 1979
- Charles-Mendel, ed. *La Legion d'Honneur et les Decorations Francais*, Paris, 1911.
- Hicks, Major James E. *French Military Weapons 1717-1938*, N. Flayderman & Co., New Milford, Connecticut, 1964
- La Cohorte. *Napoleon et la Legion d'Honneur*, La Societe d'Entraide des Membres de la Legion d'Honneur, Paris, 1968
- Musee Monetaire. *Ordres de Chevalerie et Recompenses Nationales* Administration des Monnaies et Medailles, Paris, 1956.
- Paris, W. Francklyn. *Napoleon's Legion*, Funk and Wagnall's Company, New York, 1927
- Renault, Jules. *La Legion d'Honneur et les Anciens Ordres Francais*, Societe de la Legion d'Honneur, Paris 1924
- Richardson, B.A., Hubert N.B. *A Dictionary of Napoleon and His Times* Cassell and Company, Ltd, London, 1920
- Sculfort, Lieutenant. *Decorations, Medailles, Monnaies et Cachets du Musee de l'Armee* J. Leroy & Cie, Editeurs, Paris, 1912
- Venner, Dominique. *Les Armes a Feu Francaises*, Jacques Grancher, editeur, Paris, 1979

* * *

Mr. Grabenhorst is a graduate of Willamette University, Salem, Oregon, B of A art major. A competitive swimmer and Marine Corps sergeant, he has been very active in restoration of historical commercial buildings in Oregon, serving on numerous civic and historical committees and commissions. He is a Realtor in the family firm founded in 1910, and has also been a restauranteur with his brother for the past 15 years. He collects and deals fine art and historically related collectibles. Of primary interest to him is his 20 year membership in the Orders and Medals Society of America and his current positions as a commissioner on the Oregon Secretary of State's Historic Properties Commission and as a member of the board of directors of The Napoleonic Society of America.

He dedicated his paper to his parents and his brothers, Jean and Geoffrey, and thanked his great friend Daniel Adolphe and his wife Susan for their assistance in its preparation.

Costume During The Napoleonic Wars
by Timothy Pickles, New Orleans, LA

"It is by baubles that men are lead;" or so Napoleon said when instituting the *'Legion D'Honneur*. However, this view of the human love of magnificence and glorification was exemplified most in the uniforms, both military and court, that Napoleon required his followers to wear. For all his new ideas the Emperor was enough of an 18th century man to want to join the 'club' of European monarchs and when they snubbed him his desire was to out-do them. In the army there were also very real advantages. The more gorgeously a soldier is dressed the more pride he is likley to feel in himself and his unit, the more pride he feels the better he is likely to fight. It has been truly said that nothing could be more degrading to the one nor more flattering to the other than to compare Napoleon and Hitler but in what each of them did in smartening up the uniforms and militarizing their respective countries it is instructive to look at how Hitler smartened up the WW1 uniform for the 3rd Reich and compare this with how Napoleon adapted that of the Revolutionary Army for the 1st Empire. Of course, in this comparison it is well to remember that Hitler was trying to model himself on Napoleon! Logically as the rank of the soldier got higher the uniform became more and more magnificent up to the beautiful (and hideously expensive) gala dress of a Marshal of the Empire. Napoleon, of course, adopted the simple undress uniform of a colonel of the *Chasseurs a Cheval de la Garde Imperiale* which had the effect of making him stand out against the gorgeously uniformed Imperial Staff, making him a figure that the ordinary soldier could identify with. The Little Corporal who commanded in Italy, *le*

Tondu (the Shorn One) who had been cheered round the camp fires and had the next day led them to a crushing victory over the combined armies of Austria and Russia on the field of Austerlitz. The classic image of the French Napoleonic army did not develop until around 1807. The old *habit longue* of the French infantry was refined over the period 1800-06, cut to be more form fitting, eventually the turnbacks permanently sewn down and generally made smarter. The cocked hat of the infantry which had been adopted by the Revolutionary Army as a cheap alternative to the tarleton helmet of the Royalist army was itself to give way to the familiar bell topped shako with cords and plume. The elite infantry companies and of course the infantry of the Old Guard retained the universal symbol of the elite soldier, the bearskin and epaulettes. The army was no longer *sans coulottes*. In fact, breeches and gaiters were universal although towards the end of the Empire trousers did make a re-apperance as campaign wear. Also for campaign wear many officers adopted the undress cocked hat instead of the shako as a more convenient item. The staff universally had a collapsible form of cocked hat called the *chapeau bras* (arm hat, ie, one could put it under the arm). This name stuck even when the hat crossed the Atlantic to America, to the extent that even today senior and staff officers are known as "brass hats"! The last design for the infantry was the uniform specified in the 'Bardan' regulations of 1812, not much in evidence before the campaigns of 1813, this consisted of the shako without cords and plume replaced by a pompom of company colour. The coat still had lapels but now closed with hooks and eyes down to the waist so that the lapels could be buttoned across if nessasary for campaign.

The tails were shorter, and of course the new front closure of the coat did away with the need for a waistcoat. Technically, the breeches and gaiters (though now coming just below the knee instead of just above) were retained but during the final campaigns when these uniforms were seen on the young 'Marie Louises' (who were being trained on the march in an attempt to replace the losses of Russia and Leipzig) trousers of various descriptions were not uncommon. The cavalry at the outset of the Revolution was dressed much as the infantry with the *habit longue* and cocked hat. The dragoons had a helmet, a fairly low brass peakless affair of classical style, and the hussars had made the first steps along the road to glamour. Hussars had been introduced to the French army during the campaigns of Marshal de Saxe and were originally considered the lowest of the low, wildmen with their long red nightcaps edged in fur, an animal skin thrown over their shoulder instead of a greatcoat and their rudimentary coat fastened with toggles instead of buttons. Early in the Revolution the Hussars, who had been undergoing smartening up throughout the 18th century, were seen as a glamorous unit. Perhaps because their look was so un-Royalist or perhaps because after the formation of the Consulate the First Consul had his personal bodyguard, the *Guides de Bonaparte*, dressed in Hussar fashon. Later, of course, it was this unit re-named the *Chasseurs a Cheval de la Garde Imperiale* that accompanied the Emperor's carriage and were his constant companions. As has been stated above it was the undress uniform of this regiment that Napoleon himself habitually wore. The rest of the cavalry uniforms went through much the same alterations as the infantry. The helmets, though became the real focus of attention. The Republicans had adopted classical themes which Napoleon not only continued but expanded upon, most evidently in the helmets of the dragoons and cuirassiers. The style was based on the statues of Minerva the Greek Goddess of war, hence the name of the style. In an even more overtly classical touch the cuirass was re-introduced for the heavy cavalry who were thereafter called Cuirassiers. In the old Royal Army only the 8th cavalry used the curass and then with the cocked hat. The exception to this general modernisation were the Carabineers who as the senior regiment of heavy cavalry of the line, jealously hung on to their very pre-revolutionary looking bearskins and long blue coats. However, eventually the Emperor decided that his senior troops must be "Classisized" and given the fame of the Greek looking Cuirassiers, they must moreover be Romanized! The result is now familiar to us all, the copper helmet with silver fittings (brass for other ranks) surmounted by an enormous red cheniele or caterpillar. The steel cuirass overlaid with copper (brass for other ranks) and lined with blue cloth. Interestingly the Carabineers also now had white coats, the traditional colour of the French infantry.

During the period of the Empire, although the Continental System was supposed to cut England off from all European trade, the British Empire was the only source of Indigo dye for the French uniforms so Napoleon had the idea of going back to the pre-Revolutionary colour of white; several units, including the *21me de ligne* were outfitted in white. However, the story goes that the Emperor could be surprisingly squeamish at times and at the battle of Eylau the effect of blood and gore on white uniformed troops standing in snow so sickened him that he decided to pay the black marketeers their price for the indigo. So the Carabineers became the only French unit to retain the white uniform (although the 13th Cuirassiers also wore white; they were Dutch troops). The Polish campaign brought into the Imperial Army the distinctive uniform of the Polish light horse; this uniform, which is known today universally as 'lancer', was used by a formation that, initially, was an officer corps and did not carry lances. Later, when the regiment was enlarged, Napoleon saw the value of the Polish national weapon, added some Polish regiments to his line cavalry, and converted some of his dragoon regiments to lancers. French lancers wore a uniform similar to the Poles but in their traditional green and retaining their original facing colour distinctions. Their headgear was the helmet but with the horsehair mane and houpett removed and a black bearskin chenille reminiscent of the carabineers in their *cimier*. On the field of battle then there was quite a difference between a French lancer and a Polish lancer. All the above and more aplied to the Imperial Guard which constituted an army within an army. Whatever the Line had the Guard had more of it including pay (the exception being the mamelukes who wore a uniform so elaborate and expensive that their pay was cut to help pay for it). Napoleon's fascination with the cuirass though began to get out of hand, he decided that the general officers should also wear it. Two were made; of superb workmanship in blackened steel with gold oakleaf borders and studs, crimson velvet liner and a matching helmet in cuirassier style. When Berthier appeared at Tilsit wearing it (at the Emperor's request) the rest of the marshals hooted with derisive laughter and the idea was dropped. The originals may be seen in the Museum of the *Legion d'Honneur*. And in case you were wondering, the second set was made for the Emperor, although as far as we know he never wore it, at least in public!

Perhaps the most revealing form of dress, in terms of Napoleon's ambitions for his new regime, is the dress of the Court. In spite of all the rhetoric about breaking with the past, Napoleon chose to surround himself with a court modeled directly on that of the pre-Revolutionary Kings of France. Gentlemen of the Bedchamber, Master of the Horse, Master of Ceremonies, Grand Admiral of the Empire and all the rest had their places and their uniforms. The pre-Revolutionary styles and formality emphasized the absolutism of the regime but with most of the courtiers, unfamiliar with the ceremonies they were supposed to perform, the magnificence of the dress had to cover many formal inadequacies. Of course there were some who would have no truck with these ideas, particularly Marshals Lannes (who at the coronation threw a bishop out of his seat so that he could sit down) and Augerau, but nevertheless, they both had all the required court dress. That of Marshals Lannes and Ney may be seen at the Invalides in Paris.

This necessarily brief and sketchy overview of the development of French uniforms would nonetheless be incomplete if its influence on military uniforms generaly were not mentioned. It is interesting to note that even England, the old enemy of Napoleon, succumed. By 1825 the once distinctive uniforms of 'Perfideous Albion' had become Frenchified to the extreme, infantry in bell topped shakos and long tailed coats, all the Foot Guards in bearskins and epaulettes, the 9th Light Dragoons converted to lancers in a uniform so similar to that of the Poles that they could have ridden alongside them unnoticed. Usually the world follows the military fashions of the victor. That in this instance they followed the vanquished shows the effectiveness of Napoleon's vision. Even today we can say with confidence that this was the age of the uniform.

* * *

Timothy Pickles is from Yorkshire, England, and is a technical advisor/costume designer for the film and television industry as well as being a writer on military subjects. A founder member and chairman for six years of the British Napoleonic Association in which he still commands the British Brigade, he is also a director of the Napoleonic Society of America, historical consultant to the Louisiana State Museum, and a member of the National Advisory Board of the Lousiana Council for Music and the Performing Arts. His work has included the films Tai-Pan, The Hostage of Europe, Napoleon and Josephine *and research for the Journal of the Napoleonic Association. He also wrote the chapter* Prince Murat *in David Chandler's book* Napoleon's Marshals *and is presently engaged in writing* New Orleans *for the Osprey Campaigns series. Timothy is married to an American and lives in New Orleans.*

Napoleon's Administrative Army-
His Prefects
by Robert D. Williams, Concord, MA

"Citizens, the Revolution is bound to the principles with which it began. The Revolution is ended."[1] With these words began the efforts of First Consul Bonaparte to reconcile political factions and to restore order. After the *coup d'etat* of the Eighteenth Brumaire (9, November, 1799), Bonaparte faced the dilemma of having to establish a system of authority different from those of the proceeding decade and yet which would maintain the basic principles that had cost so many French lives. The instability and disruption associated with the failures of a constitutional monarchy and a republic left only one possible solution: a fusion of the traditional structure of the Old Regime with the new ideas of the Revolution. Some way of harmonizing authority with liberty, equality and fraternity in the new regime appeared to be the only foundation upon which the First Consul could establish his power.

On February 17, 1800, First Consul Bonaparte issued a law revising the French administrative system. In place of Intendants, of legislative representatives on mission, of locally-elected directories, he instituted the rule of the prefect, directly responsible to the Minister of the Interior, and in reality, to the First Consul. The most absolute centralization, even upon the visions of generations of Capetian Monarchs, had at last been realized by an individual who was as much a fusion of the Old Regime and the Revolution as the government and society which he tried to create.

The Constitution of the year VIII adopted on 13 December, 1799 had not dealt with the organization of local administration.[2] Siéyès had described the creation of "regional Prefects" in an earlier draft of a proposed constitution.[3] The new Constitution had retained the geographic division of France in departments, a division which had been created in the waning months of 1789 by the Constituent Assembly and which had been retained by the Constitution of the year III adopted in 1795. At the time of Bonaparte's coup in 1799, there were 98 departments, "88 for the actual French territory, 9 for Belgium and Luxembourg which had been annexed in 1795, one for Geneva annexed in 1798". The French empire at its height comprised 130 departments.[4]

The law creating the prefectural organization of 17 February, 1800, provides as follows:

"There shall be in each department a prefect, a council of prefecture and a department general, which shall discharge the functions now performed by the administrations and department commissioners....The prefect alone shall be charged with the administration....The First Consul shall appoint the prefects, the councillors of prefecture, the members of the general council of the departments, the general secretary for the prefecture, the sub-prefects, the members of the district council, the mayors and deputies of the cities of more than five thousand inhabitants, the commissioners-general of police and Prefects of police in the cities in which they shall be established.'[5]

There were, however, no detailed directives on the use or application of this power provided in the law, or any definition of "administration" as to which the prefects were in charge. To remedy this situation, Lucien Bonaparte, acting as Minister of the Interior, issued a circular dated March 12, 1800, ten days after the first appointments had been announced, which reaffirmed in more concrete terms the position of the prefect as the chief administrator of the department: "Your mission...reaches all branches of internal administration....Your prerogatives embrace everything that concerns the public welfare and national prosperity, for the best interests of those whom you serve."[6]

He added that the powers of the prefect extended to "conscription, tax collections, agriculture, industry, commerce, public work, the fine arts, bridges and roads, public welfare, [and] public education."[7]

While the burdens placed on the prefect were heavy, the assistant agencies provided for by the administrative law had but limited functions. A council of prefecture dealt only with litigation which might arise when the prefect attempted to execute his duties, as for example, over the collection of taxes. A second council, the general council, convened only once a year, and then for a maximum of fifteen days. The functions of this council were limited to financial problems, as tax assessment and the report of the "conditions and needs of the department" which is sent directly to the Minister of the Interior.[8] Finally, the sub-prefect acted as the administrative head of each communal district and performed most of the duties previously executed by the "municipal administrations and cantonal commissioners".[9] It was this latter figure, therefore, who was second in power only to the prefect, while the councils were peripheral bodies by comparison.

Obviously, there was still too much for the prefect alone, and he therefore maintained a staff of subordinate administrators. For example, in the department of the Bouches-du-Rhône, the office of the prefecture employed seven bureaus in 1804. Altogether, they represent the functions and concerns outlined in Lucien's circular. A general secretariat handled petitions, correspondence, registration of laws and decrees, and supervision of the archives. A bureau of internal administration supervised commerce, education, sciences, the arts, agriculture, health, taxes, civilian hospitals, and similar institutions. There were, however, separate bureaus for public works and the national domains. The subprefecture consisting of a prefect's duties in microcosm was yet another. Finally, two which performed those functions to prove most significant and crucial for the Napoleonic regime were that of (1) finances and (2) police and military duties. The former concentrated on direct taxes, departmental expenditures, municipal expenditures and expenses and, in general, the accounts of the department. The latter supervised conscription and the multitude of lesser matters as weights and measures, paupery, the national guard, pension, power, assemblies and national festivals.[10] It has been pointed out that the Prefects were used by Bonaparte as a means of constraining individuals belonging to factions who opposed the government by means of a system of "supervised residences, a restraint on individual liberty in the name of security of the State, especially useful in isolating militant minorities, especially the former Jacobins and terrorists".[11]

The prefects, along with their attendant administrations, were uniformed.

"Bonaparte, who began to put France in uniform, equipped the prefects, subprefects and all the personnel of the prefectures and subprefectures with uniforms. For the prefects, it was a blue coat embroidered with silver at the collar, at the cuffs and at the pockets, under which there was next a white vest. The trousers were also white. A red scarf with silver fringes completed the outfit, with a hat also embroidered in silver."[12]

What was the derivation or antecedents of, or model for, this system of administration so adopted? It has survived fairly well intact to the present day and has proved to be one of the most durable of the Napoleonic institutions. The name "prefect" certainly evokes Roman antiquity, for which there was a penchant at the time.[13] As earlier stated, the name was not applied by Bonaparte, but had been used previously by Siéyès. The name "prefect" had been in fact used in Imperial Rome for a lower level provincial administrator, typically of a military character, though some had certain judicial duties.[14]

While there was a certain prestige associated with imperial antiquity, clearly the function and power of the new prefect was substantially greater than that of the Roman model. While the administrative departmental divisions established during the Revolution were retained by Bonaparte, the administrative organization and its functioning must be sharply contrasted with that created by the revolutionary governments. During the Revolution, there were locally elected councils but there was no executive connection between the local groups and the central government.[15] As Alfred Cobban points out in his seminal article entitled *Local Government during the French Revolution* there are four basic reasons for the failure of local government as created by the revolutionary assemblies:

1. The lack of an executive liaison as described;

2. The lack of fundamental powers including the ability to adequately finance the government locally;

3. Lack of cooperation and the conflicts created among the local bodies because of different constituencies; and

4. The rivalry between the revolutionary municipalities and the generally more conservative departmental directories.[16]

The administrative organization headed by the prefect under Bonaparte effectively cured all of these ills by providing an extremely centralized and controlled structure. An astute memorialist of that time, Etienne-Denis Pasquier, commented that local government during the Revolution included "a number of petty officials, who were both worthless and incapable, and at whose mercy the administration of the departments and *arrondissments* had been for the past ten years. They were all the more inclined to make the weight of their authority felt, because they had almost all of them sprung from the lowliest strata of society".[17] While this may be an overly biased and over generalized comment, nonetheless, the point is made.

By contrast, the centralized administration of France by Bonaparte draws more completely and directly on the system of intendants of the *Ancien Régime*. It has been brilliantly described by Alexis de Tocqueville.

"The Intendant was a young man of humble extraction, who had still his way to make and was never a native of the province to which he was posted. He did not obtain his office by purchase, by right of birth, or by election, but was chosen by the government from amongst the junior members of the Council and he was always liable to dismissal. In the official jargon of the time he was described as a *commissaire départi*, because he had been 'detached' from the Council to act as its provincial agent. Most of the powers possessed by the Council itself were vested in him and he was entitled to use them as he thought fit. Like those of the Council these were both administrative and judicial; he corresponded directly with Ministers and was sole executant of all the measures enacted by the government in the province to which he had been posted.

Under him and appointed by him were the officials known as 'subdelegates', one for each canton, and he could dismiss them at will. The Intendant was usually a man who had recently been raised to noble rank, the subdelegate always a commoner. Nevertheless, within his smaller sphere of influence the latter - - like the Intendant as regards the *généralité* (administrative district) as a whole - was a plenary representative of the government. He was subordinate to the Intendant in the same way as the latter was subordinate to the Minister of State."[18]

As we will discuss later, even the system developed for the training of subsequent cadres of administrative functionaries created by Bonaparte was very similar to that created by the Bourbons for the training of Intendants and other administrative officials. Similarity of function and power is truly brought home by a study of Turgot's experiences as Intendant of Limoges and who later became Controller-General of France from 1774-6 under Louis XVI.[19]

Who were the personnel of the prefectures under Bonaparte as Consul and then Napoleon as Emperor? Over thirty years ago, Professor Crane Brinton, then McLane Professor of Ancient and Modern History at Harvard, suggested to me that a study of the backgrounds of the personnel of the prefectures of Napoleon was a topic still not adequately pursued. In his doctoral thesis "The Jacobins" published in the thirties, he had made the statement that "man after man assumes an appointed position under the Directory, and ends up as a Napoleonic official — prefect, subprefect, mayor, judge. Napoleon was as indebted to the Jacobin government for civil administration as he was to the Revolutionary Armies for his military leaders.[20] But he had never pursued a study to confirm this general statement. The following statistical analysis of the personnel of the prefects, in abreviated form, is based in large part upon five or six months I then spent pursuing this topic.[21]

The basis for the study were the 257 men who served as prefects from the original appointments of March 2, 1800, through the calendar year 1812.22

Since by law and by personality, Bonaparte and then Napoleon controlled the appointments to the prefectures, it is informative to observe the nature of these appointments and to analyze the probable basis for them.

The first appointments of 1800 did not solely represent the

choices of Bonaparte even though the law of February 17, 1800, which had established the prefectural system of administration, specifically empowered the First Consul alone to appoint these administrative officials. Bonaparte, Corsican by birth, and military by occupation, did not possess the broad knowledge of available man power which others had acquired by wide political experience and numerous acquaintances during the proceeding decade.[23] He had been a marginal figure in political circles during the years of upheaval and prior to that too young and taciturn to have developed a knowledge of Old Regime administrators. The First Consul, therefore, necessarily relied upon the judgment of others.

Six men formed the essential sources of recommendation in the initial selection of prefects in March, 1800: Lucien Bonaparte, Napoleon's brother, as Minister of the Interior, Jacque-Claude Beugnot, Lucien's secretary and then himself prefect of the department of the Seine-Inferiéure as a reward for his services in the nominating process, Cambacérès and Lebrun, the Second and Third Consuls respectively, the former a regicide and the latter an old royalist, Talleyrand, with his tremendous knowledge of men of both the Old Regime and the Revolution, having himself played a significant role in both epochs, and finally, General Clarke at the head of a special bureau whose main function was the gathering and assimilation of information on candidates for public office.[24] All eccept Lebrun had been men of influence and activity in the Revolution. Each made his recommendation or commented upon that of his colleagues, both notations appearing on the great chart "attached to the first minute concerning the nomination of the prefects".[25] The significant factor, as seen from these tables, remained in the column entitled "decision" - under which the final selections are crudely penned in the hand of the First Consul. Bonaparte retained the power of ultimate choice, even initially.

The legacy of the Revolution cannot be denied, for it is a heritage which influences the entire Napoleonic epoch, which, in so many aspects, is but the inevitable culmination of the preceding tumultuous decade. And so in personnel: of the 257 prefects appointed from 1800 through 1812, 172, or approximately 68%, were men who had been employed by the Revolutionary governments. The rest were of the new generation, too young to have taken part in the Revolution, or were foreign-born, or were too obscure to have made a mark during this period. Bonaparte leaned heavily on the parliamentarians for filling the new positions created by the Constitution of the Year VIII. One third of the men appointed as prefects from March 2, 1800 through the last months of 1812 had sat in one or more of the Revolutionary assemblies. Fifty-five of these 85 ex-deputies were appointed in 1800 alone. The majority of the others were appointed before 1803, while only four were appointed after 1805. The first years of the Consulate, therefore, in fact the years in which the greatest number of Prefects per year were appointed, saw the major influx of the men of revolutionary parliamentary background.

Most of the former legislators had been members of the Constituent Assembly, or the Legislative Corps of the Directory. In other words, those two bodies that marked the beginning and the end of the Revolution. Men of the prefectures, some 28 in number, who had sat in the Constituent Assembly were the moderate men of this first revolutionary assembly. One general indication of this is the fact that out of the 18 who served only in this legislative body, eleven emigrated, retired from political life, or were imprisoned under the radical revolutionary regimes.

Were there extremists? Of the 85 ex-deputies appointed to the prefectures, only 23, or 27% had sat in the Convention, the assembly which presided through the Terror. Sixteen of these received the nomination as prefect in 1800. None was appointed after 1805. On analysis of the activities of these men who sat in the Convention, only approximately three could be identified as true extremists. And, it is significant that these three men, the extremists, would all serve the prefectures of newly annexed departments. Their Revolutionary reputations would there be at a minimum, and yet their education, experience and special knowledge did not go unused by a regime in need of administrative talent. The largest number of parliamentarians to serve the prefectures sat in the assemblies of the Directory. Fifty, or 59%, of the total number of prefects with experience in the Revolutionary assemblies, served the Directory in this capacity, but some of these had had prior parliamentary experience as well.

Bonaparte attempted to bind all parties to his regime by a system of recruitment, but with a few brilliant exceptions, he chose the moderate examples from these parties. The extremes, outright royalism and committed Jacobinism, were very sparsely represented. More important, even these were capable of compromise. Vieuville, an old royalist, became Chamberlain to an Emperor rejected by the legitimate thrones of Europe; Quinette, an extreme Jacobin, reinstituted an anachronistic symbol of royalism to greet a First Consul about to make mockery of the principle of popular sovereignty.[26] Pasquier, in his memoirs, observes that the total credit for political careers open to talent without regard to past affiliations with respect to filling of offices of all kinds, including the prefects and subprefects, belongs to Bonaparte.[27]

Historians have also argued as to whether or not subsequent appointments to the prefectures reflected a change in Napoleon's political selection. For example, Jacques Godechot asserts that after 1805, Napoleon, substituting loyalty for competence, recruited especially from the "victims" of the initial revolution, by which he means the royalist-aristocratic political elements.[28] Conversely, Alphonse Aulard comments that "it is incorrect to claim Napoleon, in appointing new prefects, had chosen any differently during the Empire than he had during the Consulate. The selections of the Emperor were not more conservative than those of the First Consul and there is no political tendency illustrated by these selections".[29]

In terms of information obtained in varying degrees for 73% (186) of the 257 Prefects under examination, 47% (88) were by origins or status of the nobility, either sword or robe, while 52% (95) were of the bourgeoisie: both represent the heritage of the Old Regime. Less than 2% (3) were of lower-class origins, while on their own status they belong at least to the petty bourgeoisie. There were no peasants. When one views the composition of these three categories, the overwhelming preponderance rests in the highest strata of 18th century French society. Most of those prefects who represent the bourgeoisie, however, were within the upper half of that class, either by social origins or contemporary status: 71% (67) were above middle bourgeoisie; most of whom can be truly classified as the high bourgeoisie; 28% (26) were of the middle bourgeoisie; less than 2% (2) were of the petty bourgeoisie, not including the three noted previously.

The highest stratum of the Old Regime reflected in the personnel of the Napoleonic centralization consisted of the nobility, both robe and sword, that is judicial representatives and old aristocrats, respectively. This class did not "remain suppressed" in either the Consulate or the Empire within the ranks of the prefects.[30] While the Constitution of the Year VIII had reasserted the stringent laws against the *émigrés* in order to quiet perpetual fears of those possessing national lands, the confiscated lands of the *émigrés* the laws with regard to the deposed were gradually relaxed even under the Consulate. On March 2, 1800 the same day significantly that the first nominations to the prefectures were announced, a consular decree pardoned the *émigrés* of the Constituent Assembly who could prove that they had not subverted the principals of this body during their exile.[31] Finally, in a *Senatus-Consulte* of 1802, the First Consul declared a general amnesty.[32] Even more, the government not only permitted them to return to France, but also gave them employment in its service. Approximately 20% of the nobility in the prefectures were of the robe, and the majority of these were high robe officials, sovereign court personnel of the Old Regime.

While the men representing the nobility of the sword, that is, the old aristocracy were present, these were not the impoverished nobility of the 18th century who needed employment with Napoleon in order to survive economically. Quite the contrary: from those of the oldest houses through and including the youngest members of the new generation serving under Napoleon in the latter years of the Empire, the dominant characteristic was extreme wealth. This general stratification of the prefects socially portrays a preponderance of the upper classes in French society.

Historians have argued over whether or not there was a shift during the Consulate to the Empire from middle class representation to a greater preponderance of nobles culminating during the apogee of the Empire, 1810 and 1811, in that phenomenon which historians have termed "the aristocratic reaction". Simply, they mean that the old nobility, along with Napoleon's own creation, the imperial nobility, gained ascendance in the prominent positions under the Empire.

Actually, more nobles gained appointment to the prefectures during the Consulate, than during the Empire. However, in proportion to the number appointed, more nobles assumed the chief administrative office during the Empire than those of other classes.

Of the 257 prefects appointed from 1800 through 1812, only 83, or 32% became prefects after 1804. So it was a stable administrative system in terms of its personnel. The fact that in seven years of a era which saw almost ceaseless foreign wars and ongoing internal economic crisis there should be so little turnover within the main domestic structure of rule is evidence of this stability. The Consulate was a regime of construction: the great shifting of personnel that occurred was only natural in the formation of a new regime. The Empire presented few changes in administrative personnel. Of those 109 prefects appointed in the course of 1800, 30 still held the office of prefect in 1810, in spite of the great readjustments of 1801 and 1802, not to mention the more often noted replacement of personnel in 1810.

The comparative age levels present one indication of this phenomenon of relative stability.[33] The average age of the first appointees directly following the law of 1800 is 43 years, the same as the overall average for all twelve years under examination. However, the average age of the prefects in office in 1810 is 46 years, even though the appointees have become younger, on the average, as the years passed. The higher average age of those in office in the later year is the reflection of a basically stable system as it normally aged.

Re-appointment is the prime factor in the explanation for the circulation of many prefects. The use of the prefectures as a reservoir for upper-level administrative personnel was, in fact an important procedure in the Napoleonic Regime.

But were these men competent to do the job for which they were appointed? Having reviewed the extensive scope of their function in office for which they were responsible, did these appointees have the requisite skills? Competency seems to be the common characteristic and the real driving force behind the appointments. These were truly qualified men for the most part who bring to bear real technical expertise in a variety of areas and strengths.

The majority of the prefects, representing those generations born in the years 1748 to 1768, were men who had established themselves successfully under the Old Regime. The upper-class preponderance and economic substance of the greater number and the upward mobility of the others indicate that these men were not failures. Quite the contrary: the administrators, lawyers, magistrates and army officers of the Old Regime who appeared in the prefectures had held positions of influence in 18th century France. Prior to their appointment to the prefectures, 137, or approximately 50%, of these men had pursued a career in the bureaucracy, the army, the bar, or the bench under the Bourbons. Of this group, approximately 14% were bureaucrats, 25% lawyers, 25% magistrates and 36% army officers. Other professions included eleven teachers or professors, eight writers, four great merchants, three clerics, two doctors, a road surveyor, a protestant pastor and a glass works craftsman.

But it was the Revolution which prepared them for Napoleon. All of the 21 bureaucrats of the Old Regime held at some time in that chaotic epoch an administrative position, while at least one-half sat in one or more of the Revolutionary Assemblies. Twenty-three of the 34 prefects who had been lawyers, practicing in either the lower courts or the *parlements* sat in one or more of the assemblies of the Revolution, while the 11 men who did not all served in administrative capacities during that period. Of the 36 magistrates, 12 continued in judicial duties, while 16 others took administrative functions. Only 11 of these men did not sit in one of these assemblies. Only 16 of the 46 representatives from the royal army remained within a purely military position and even six of these held administrative positions for short durations. The remaining thirty all gained either administrative or parliamentary experience from the Revolution. Finally, of the others — the scattering of intellectuals, merchants, doctors and clerics, whose main careers prior to the Revolution lay outside the four major divisions, all without exception attained some measure of administrative, parliamentary, or technical experience during the Revolution or the Napoleonic Regime before they assumed the duties of departmental administration. Nevertheless, the prefects of the Revolutionary generation had not been, in general, the formulators of Revolutionary policy, but rather its executors.

The ex-deputies had served the technical committees in one or more of the four assemblies. Others had been local and departmental administrators or judicial officers, while still others had served in the army. Moreover, a common occurrence was the combination of administrative and one or more technical skills in their backgrounds.

According to Beugnot, Napoleon in 1811 at the height of his power expressed a regret that the men of the Revolutionary generation would vanish simultaneously from their positions of power and influence, leaving a great void. He relied heavily upon the men tempered by the Revolution in establishing his power and continuing in its administration. Upon Beugnot's consolation that there was a rich reservoir of skill to be found among the masters of requests and the auditors of the Council of State, the Emperor could not agree. In his mind, there was something about those who had experienced the great upheaval of the preceding decade which could never be reproduced. And it was this vague quality upon which he so much depended.[34]

In order to provide the training ground for new bureaucrats, in lieu of the experience obtained by the Revolution as that generation was waning, Napoleon created a program of "auditors" to the Council of State. The functions of this particular office, created in March of 1803, make it apparent that it was to provide a reservoir for higher administrative officials, especially the prefects. This system of training administrators was similar to that employed by the Bourbons, as they recruited most of their Intendants from among the masters of request which served a similar function in the Controller-General's office under the Monarchy.

The auditor acted as an intermediary between each section of the Council of State — finances, civil and criminal legislation, war, navy and interior — and the respective minister of each corresponding department of the government, for whom the auditor presented and defended specific ministerial proposals. He also served on missions to various parts of the Empire to insure the execution of imperial decrees, much as the Commissioners of the Executive Directory.

In general, the administrative system was stable during the period 1800 to 1812. In 1810, there appeared the same professional representation as in 1800. The majority of the men in the system still reflected the heritage of the Revolution. But Napoleon had created an institution which provided for a continuation of administrative skill, for a new reservoir from which he could appoint his prefects.

What Napoleon had created was a "cadre of technocrats", professional functionaries meant to serve him. With minor modification, this system of civil administration exists in France to this day.

Footnotes

1. *Correspondence de Napoleon Ier* (Paris, 1858-1870), VI, No. 4422

2. Vandal, Albert, *L'Avenement de Bonaparte*, (Paris, 1907), Vol. II p. 189.

3. Ibid., p. 189.

4. Godechot, Jacques, *Les Institutions de la France sous La Revolution et L'Empire*, (Paris, 1968), pp. 586-587.

5. *Bulletin des lois*, 3e Serie, I, no 115; Anderson, Frank M., *The Constitution and other Select Documents Illustrative of the History of France*, (Minn., 1904), pp. 285-287.

6. Arch. nat. AB XIX 348 (legs Beugnot), quoted in Dejean, Etienne, *Un prefet du Consulat: Jacques-Claude Beugnot*, (Paris, 1907), p. 92.

7. Pontiel, Felix, *Napoleon, Ier et l'Organisation autoritaire de le Frfance*, (Paris 1956), p. 48.

8. *Bulletin des lois*, No. 17, Titre II, Sect. I/II.

9. *Ibid.*

10. Saint-Yves, Georges and Fournier, Joseph, *Le department des Bouches-des-Rhone de 1800 a 1810*, (Paris, 1899), p. 55-57.

11. Bergeron, Louis, *France Under Napoleon*, (Princeton, 1981), p. 9.

12. Savant, Jean, *Les Prefets de Napoleon*, (Paris, 1958), p. 24.

13. *Ibid.*, p. 21.

14. Arnold, W.T., *The Roman System of Provincial Administration*

to the Accession of Constantine the Great, Revised by E.S. Boucher, 3rd ed., (Oxford, 1914), p. 68-69.

15. Cobban, Alfred, "Local Government during the French Revolution," in *Aspects of the French Revolution*, (London, 1968), p. 118: *Memoirs of Chancellor Pasquier*, Duc d'Audiffret-Pasquier, ed., (London, 1893), Vol. I, p. 158.

16. Cobban, *op. cit.* n. 15, pp. 119-123.

17. *Memoirs of Chancellor Pasquier*, op. cit. n. 15, p. 159.

18. De Tocqueville, Alexis, T*he Old Regime and the French Revolution*, Gilbert, trans., Anchor Edition (NY, 1955), pp. 35-36.

19. See, Stephens, W. Walker, *The Life and Writings of Turgot*, (NY, 1971 repr. of 1895 ed.), pp. 25-76.

20. Brinton, Clarence Crane, *The Jacobins*, (Cambride, 1930, repr. NY, 1961), p. 231.

21. The following analysis of the sprefectoral personnel is based upon that study, an unpuiblished 1961 thesis of the author entitled "The Political, Social and Professional Origins of Napoleon's Prefects (1800-1812)" on file in Widener Library, Harvard Un iversity.

22. The names were compiled from the *Almanach national* (- - imperial) an VIII - 1813 and cross-checked with Jean Savant, *Les prefets de Napoleon*, pp. 218-321. Appendix I to this paper contains a list of the 257 prefects which served as the basis for the study and of the information contained in the following pages of this paper.

23. Lefebvre, Georges, *Napoleon*, (Paris, 1953, 4th ed.). p. 83; cf. Durand, Charles, *Etudes sur le Conseil d'Etat Napoleonien*, (Paris, 1949), p. 269.

24. Dejean, Etienne, *Un prefet du Consulat, Jacques-Claude Beugnot*, (Paris, 1907), pp. 61-75. General Clarke was head of the *Service de renseignements de Bonaparte*. See Savant, op. cit. p. 217.

25. De jean, *op. cit.* n. 24, (opposite p. 76) includes facsimile of three pages of this minute from the first nomination, the original of which can be found in Arch. nat. A.F. IV 8 pl. 33.

26. This is reference to the incident noted by Bourriene in which the town of Amiens, the *chef-lieu* of Quinette's department (the Somme) presented Bonaparte, in Juhne of 1803 on his entrance to the town, with a pair of swans, an ancient custom in welcoming the

French monarchs to Picardie. L.A.F. de Bourrienne, *Memoirs of Napoleon Bonaparte*, Ed. R.W. Phipps. Rev. ed. (New York, 1890), II, 197; Auguste Kuscinski, *Dictionnaire des conventionnels* (Paris, 1916-1919), 514.

27. *Memoirs of Chancellor Pasquier*, op. cit; n. 15, p. 159.
28. Godechot, Jacques, *op. cit.*, n. 4, 1951 ed., p. 511.
29. Aulard, Alphonse, "La centralisatrion Napoleoniennes les prefets." *Études et lecons sur la Révolution francaise*, 7e serie, (Paris, 1913), p. 130.
30. Leo Gershoy, *The French Revolution and Napoleon* (New York, 1933), p. 459. He comments that " the old nobility remained suppressed..." This is not confirmed by statistics with reference to the prefects.
31. *Bulletin des Lois*, No. 8, Arrete 60, Art. I.
32. Lefebvre, *op. cit.*, n. 23, p. 134.
33. The statistics on age are based on 82 percent of the 257 prefects. The youngest prefect of those whose birth dates are known was Camus-Dumartroy, appointed in 1810 at age 24, while the oldest, Baude, appoinited in 1809, was 81. Both are extremes, for while there are several (4%) of age 26-29 years, and several (3%) in their sixties, the great age blocks represent men in their middle thirties through and including those in their middle fifties. The median age, 43, correlates exactly with the average.
34. *Memoires du Comte Beugnot*, Le Comte Albert Beugnot, ed., 2nd ed. (Paris, 1868), Vol. I, pp. 459-460.

◆ ◆ ◆

Bob Williams is a general corporate and securities lawyer practicing in Boston, Massachusetts and has been a member of the NSA and its Secretary since 1985. He has been collecting books and researching and writing on Napoleon for nearly 40 years, with a special interest in Napoleonic institutions and the members of the period. Bob graduated from Harvard in 1961, magna cum laude, Phi Beta Kappa, where he majored in the history of France since 1461, writing his thesis on Napoleon's prefects. Bob and his family live in Concord, MA.

Napoleon—The Name and The Saint
by F. J. Dello Stritto, Bensalem, PA

"My fortune is not attached to the name of 'Bonaparte', but to that of 'Napoleon'" — 30 January 1806

A none-too-subtle reminder to his siblings of just who was in charge [3][1]. Napoleon had seven brothers and sisters, all with common, or at least unremarkable names. In order of birth, they are Giuseppe (Joseph), Luciano (Lucien), Maria Anna (Elisa), Luigi (Louis), Maria Paola (Pauline), Maria Annunziata (Caroline) and Girolamo (Jerome). In either Italian or French, the names are hardly unusual. Joseph, Lucien and Jerome were named for family members, Louis for his godfather. In Corsica as in any Roman Catholic country of the time, most girls were named "Maria", and became known by their second names or nicknames. Only Napoleon, the second child, received a quite unique name.

Napoleonic literature teems with speculations on the source of his greatness, on what made him the premiere man of his era. His success has been attributed, often with scanty proof, to everything from lefthandedness (he wasn't) to neurosis (who isn't?). Was he, as various writers contend or imply, driven by a Napoleonic Complex, or a Joseph Complex, or a Lucien Complex, or rebellion against his father or the morbid fear that he would share his father's early death? Were his actions and judgment influenced by any of the numerous syndromes, diseases and abnormalities proposed? A minor stone left unturned in this scavanger hunt is one undoubted oddity—his name.

During his youth in Corsica, surrounded by intimate family and friends, he had no idea that his name was unusual. His family dubbed him "Rabulione" [9] (slang for "troublemaker", it rhymes with "Napoleone"). Mediterranean peoples delight in satirizing their sonorous names.

At age 9 Napoleone Buonaparte arrived at the Brienne military school. He did not mix well at all—most classmates were older, wealthier and French. His new nickname [7], "paille au nez" ("straw in the nose", it almost rhymes) was intended and taken as a school boy's taunt. Napoleon would be aware for the remainder of his life that his name itself was distinctive. On St. Helena, he still occasionally commented on it.

Napoleon was never shy about his name. During his lifetime, with his full consent and sometimes at his decree, five nieces and nephews were named for him, as well as offspring of his staff and aides, and "one and one half" of his sons. The cruel joke of the time was that Napoleon was only half sure that Leon Denuelle was his son, and so only gave him half his name. By imperial decree, orphans of French soldiers killed at Austerlitz could add "Napoleon" to their given names [3]. All his vassal monarchs appended "Napoleon" to their titles (much as "Caesar" was used in Roman times). Hence the kings of Spain, Holland, Westphalia and Naples, and the viceroy of Italy were officially addressed as Joseph Napoleon, Louis Napoleon, Jerome Napoleon, Louis Napoleon, Joachim Napoleon and Eugene Napoleon. His name had a special peculiarity, according to Las Cases [10]:

"The archbishop who confirmed him, manifesting his astonishment at the name of Napoleon, said he did not know of any such saint, and that there was no such name in the calendar; the boy quickly replied that that could be no rule, since there were an immense number of saints, and only 365 days."

The boy Napoleon was quite right—the Roman Catholic Church then recognized about 2,700 saints and 20,000 martyrs. Seventeen years later the calendar was changed; a "St. Napoleon" was given a feast day, a *fête*. St. Napoleon's inclusion in the Imperial calendar is often portrayed an an example of an unbridled ego. St. Napoleon's Day may well not have been Napoleon's idea, but he seized on it as one of many devices useful in establishing a new monarchy and restoring the social fabric of France.

Early Napoleons

"Napoleon" and its variations[2] descend from "neo poli", meaning "new city" or "new town". New settlements under the Greeks or Romans, as under any settlers, were often named, literally, "New Town". Over the millenia, more distinctive names were adopted; Naples (Napoli) is the only major city to retain a form of this original name. The similarity between the words "Napoleonic" and "Neapolitan" is not coincidental.

As a name for persons, it has been in use since antiquity. All surviving knowledge of the Christian martyr Neapolus is contained in a single paragraph in the Roman Martyrology (published in 598 under Pope Gregory, updated in 1749):

> *2 May: At Rome the holy martyrs Saturnius, Neopolus, Germanicus and Celestine, who after much suffering were thrown into prison, where they found rest in the Lord.*

The Martyrology does not record the year. Other religious or historical figures named Neopolus or something similar also existed. Some of the biographical details attributed during the Empire to St. Napoleon may not have been total fiction, but taken from various arcane legends.

A Napoleone was a legendary founder or patron of the Orsini family of medieval Italy. The Orsinis popularized "Napoleone" as a baptismal name. Cardinal Napoleone Orsini (1263-1342) played a role in the power struggles between the Pope and the Holy Roman Emperor (the Guelph/Ghibelline conflicts) and was a sometimes ally of the poet Dante. Through their generations long involvement with the Guelph and Ghibelline, the Orsinis were also instrumental in spreading the name "Bonaparte". When a person, family or village backed the right faction, a powerful force like the Orsini could declare them "good parties" or "good people"—"buonapartes". Even today among Italian Americans, complimenting someone as "good people" is common practice.[3]

"Napoleone" became in the Mediterranean what its cousins "Newton" and "Neuburgh" are in English and German—common family names and uncommon, somewhat aristocratic sounding first names. Various Napoleones in Corsican history are Napoleone

Zomellini, a galley commander; Napoleone dalle Vie, a soldier, and Napoleone Lomellino, a commissioner of Ajaccio [7]. This Napoleone stood as godfather to Sebastiano Bonaparte, Napoleon's great grandfather, and probably brought the name into the Bonaparte family.

Naming Among the Bonaparte Males

Among Mediterranean peoples, a son is almost never named for his father (unless the father dies before the son's birth), and only infrequently for his godfather. An oldest son is named for his paternal grandfather; subsequent sons usually for other family members, often those recently deceased. Families with many sons might be creative. Likewise, when these many sons have their own sons, the first born males may not all be named for the common grandfather. But they may—an Italian family with a handful of first cousins of the same name is not uncommon.

In the 18th century, these "rules" were quite consistently followed. They are a common, probably prevailing practice today. For many generations, the Bonapartes of Corsica practiced them, as the partial genealogy below shows:

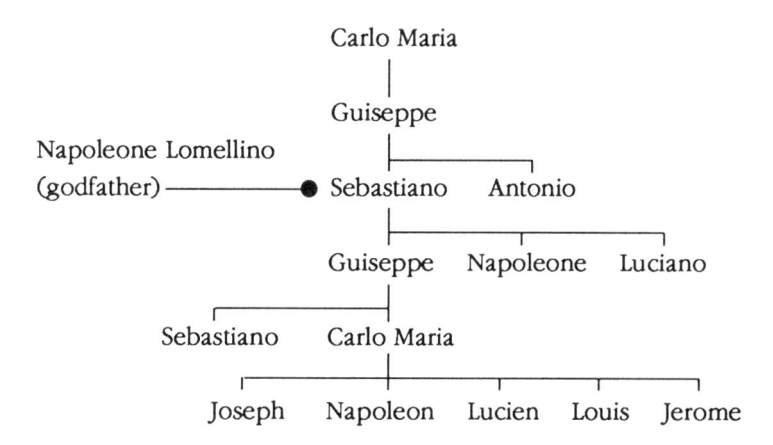

```
                        Carlo Maria
                             |
                        Guiseppe
Napoleone Lomellino          |
(godfather) ————————————● Sebastiano    Antonio
                             |
                    ┌────────┼────────┐
                Guiseppe   Napoleone  Luciano
                             |
              ┌──────────────┤
         Sebastiano      Carlo Maria
                             |
              ┌──────┬───────┼───────┬───────┐
          Joseph  Napoleon  Lucien  Louis  Jerome
```

Carlo, Napoleon's father, named his first three sons for the Bonapartes of the preceding generation. Jerome was named for his maternal grandfather; and Louis for his godfather, Louis Marbeuf. Comte Marbeuf was a French-appointed governor of Corsica, and an ally and patron of the Bonapartes [7]. The double honor of being both namesake and godfather shows the importance Carlo placed on his friendship (and also supported rumors that Marbeuf was indeed Louis' father; Carrington [7] convincingly refutes them).

Giuseppe, Carlo's father, named his sons for his father and great grandfather (bypassing his grandfather and namesake). Sebastiano, Napoleon's great grandfather, gave his first two sons the names of his father and godfather.

Napoleon broke tradition by naming his first legitimate son for himself. At the time he was more concerned with perpetuating a new dynasty than with Corsican customs. But he too was steeped in the traditions. Napoleon II's full name (Napoleon Francis Joseph Charles) includes those of both Napoleon's and Maria Louise's father and grandfather. Leon Denuelle's full name, rarely used, was Charles Leon—so Napoleon did indeed name his first born for his own father.

Towards "Napoleon Bonaparte"

Young Napoleon was not at all sure of the course of his life. In addition to his duties as a young military officer, he pursued a part-time literary career, planned to write a comprehensive history of Corsica and dabbled in Corsican politics. With some brilliant exceptions, such as his heroic performance at Toulon, he did none of these particularly well. His internal indecision may have contributed to his generally poor health, and his tinkering with his name. From signatures on his correspondence [3], the evolution may be approximated as:

> before 1785: Napoleone Buonaparte
> 1785-1787: Napoleon De Buonaparte
> 1788-1795: Napoleon Buonaparte
> after 1795: Napoleon Bonaparte

Sinister and ambitious motives have been attributed to his "gallicizing" of his name, but he never did more than add or subtract two letters. His original name was not "Nabulio", though a priest writing in Latin might so spell it[4]; and it might sound that way when pronounced by Corsicans. Given the turbulence of the times, and the fluidity of 18th century name spellings in general, the changes are insignificant. In the first mention of Napoleon on the *Moniteur* (7 December 1793, after the siege of Toulon) he was "Citizen Bona-Parte" [13]. Both "Napoleone" and "Buonaparte" had several commonly used spellings. "Buonaparte" was used by his father Carlo. His uncle Luciano, living in the same house at the same time, favored "Bonaparte". The diversity was not too rare in Italian households.

His name, however, is perhaps a small part of an amazing transformation in early 1796. Within a few weeks, Napoleon forever settled on his name, abandoned his literary career, married Josephine, embarked on the 1st Italian campaign, and exchanged ill-health for enormous energy and stamina (though he continued to look unhealthy for at least another year). All are indications of a young man resolving his doubts and pursuing his destiny.

That destiny soon brought incredible success and power. Lucien (widely considered unreliable) relates that Napoleon paused on the very threshold of that power to ponder if "Napoleon" were suitable for what he foresaw. The following conversation allegedly transpired in 1803 [1]:

Napoleon: "It's a name that doesn't sound well in French. Besides, it's an Italian name. Let Mamma call me 'Bonaparte' like everyone else—above all not 'Buonaparte', that would be worse than 'Napolion'. But no, let her say that 1st Consul or just the Consul. Yes I like that best. But 'Napolion', always this 'Napolion'—it irritates me."

Lucien: "All the same, 'Napolion', in French 'Napoleon', is a very fine name. There's a grandeur about it."

Napoleon: "You think so?"

Lucien: "Something imposing."

Napoleon: "You think so?"

Lucien: "Even majestic."

Joseph: "Indeed."

Napoleon: "You think so, too? Enfin, it is my name. I admit that it has more solemnity than 'Bonaparte', and Napoleon has the advantage of being new."

Lucien: "If you'll allow me, I stand for the name 'Napoleon'. A new great man, and a new great name!"

But the new great man could not have changed his name even if he had wanted too. It now had a life of its own. Napoleon's incredible rise to power inspired peoples everywhere, who spread his name and legend. Explorers named discoveries for him (in Australia and the Pacific Northwest). Composers named symphonies (Beethoven reneged, Paganini did not). Astronomers named stars (British astronomers countered by naming the same stars "Nelson", neither name took root). After the Egyptian campaign "Napoleon" was widely thought to mean "lion of the desert"—not quite achievable in Greek.[5] Also from Egypt came a legend of "St. Napoleon", an alleged 4th century martyr from Alexandria, executed by the emperor Diocletian. The allusion to Alexander was clear, as was the inference that an avenger had come to overthrow the tyranny which had destroyed his namesake.

The "Birth" of St. Napoleon

Just how the notion of a St. Napoleon first arose is uncertain. Perhaps it was foisted on the people by the Consulate and the Church. Perhaps it simply welled from a hero-worshipping populace. Many writers contend that, while negotiating the Concordat, Napoleon and the Church hatched the idea. Quite possibly, but evidence is circumstantial—the timing is about right, and to complete the Concordat the Pope offered and accepted many concessions.

Circumstantial evidence supports another view, as well. During the Consulate, Napoleon was not, at least outwardly, seeking deification. He was careful that he not be seen as personally too ambitious and that his star not rise too quickly. He was afterall deep in delicate negotiations not only with the Church, but also England and coalition allies. In 1800, an anonymous pamphlet appeared entitled, "A Parallel Between Caesar, Cromwell and Bonaparte" [1]. It blatantly urged that Napoleon be named king. A crown may well have already been in his plans, but Napoleon was enraged. He had the author tracked down—none other than his brother Lucien! Thus began the tempestuous falling out between the two brothers. The pamphlet was one reason Lucien did not attend the 1804 coronation he had foreseen (alas, the chief cause was a woman). So, at about the time that St. Napoleon appeared, Napoleon was downplaying rather than promoting his celebrity.

Regardless of its source, the saint had immediate uses, and was soon embraced by both Napoleon and the Church. According to O'Meara [11], Napoleon, on St. Helena, explained:

> *"St. Napoleon ought to be very much obliged to me, and do everything in his power for me in the world to come. Poor fellow; nobody knew him before. He had not even a day in the calendar. I got him one, and persuaded the Pope to give him the 15th of August, my birthday."*

> *This lighthearted remark cannot be taken at face value. It was made during what O'Meara calls a "jocular conversation". In such a mood, Napoleon hardly constrained himself to the facts. He once teased young Betsy Balcombe that he was indeed the man who burned Moscow.*

> *Another voice from St. Helena was Count de Las Cases, who writes: "Napoleon never observed his festival-day until after the Concordat: his patron saint was a stranger to the French Calendar, and even where his name is recorded, the date of his festival is a matter of uncertainty. The Pope, however, fixed it for the 15th of August, which was at once the Emperor's birthday, and the day of the signing of the Concordat."*

Most of these facts are incorrect. The Concordat was signed in July 1801, and became effective in April 1802, though it came to be celebrated on the Emperor's birthday. Napoleon had no patron saint until, from somewhere, one was invented.

But the Concordat did indeed return saints' days to the French calendar. Giving a patron saint to the man responsible was an appropriate, though generous reward. St. Napoleon's Day first appeared as a feast day (16 August or 28 Thermidor, the day after Napoleon's birthday) in the 1802 edition of France's *Almanac Nationale* [15]. In August 1802 a plebiscite on the Consulate was resoundingly approved, giving an air of official celebration to the *fête* that followed.

New Saints for Old

Napoleon had noble tasks before him. A decade of revolution and war had badly eroded the social order and fabric of France, and he set about to rebuild them. The most lasting results were the Concordat and the Code Napoleon (yet another success bearing his name). He also passed many lesser known acts towards the same goal. In 1803 a new law [16] restricted names given to newborns to those of historical or religious figures, and empowered the government to change any name deemed improper (still law in France and occasionally enforced). The First Consul enacted the law not because of his own unusual name. In France of the 1790's, as to a lesser degree in 1960's America, naming practices underwent drastic changes, with original, sometimes outlandish results. The "*Incroyables et Merveilleuses*" movement is remembered mainly for its rather comical influence on fashion, but it affected other phases of everyday life. The first Consul's act, a minor defeat for civil liberties, attempted to restore the established traditions.

One of Napoleon's first official acts as head of state was to abolish a national "holiday"—21 January, the date of Louis XVI's execution in 1793. The day was not celebrated, but was officially observed. By 1800, the chief holiday of revolutionary France, Bastille Day (14 July), with its memories of the Terror, invoked as much dread as joy [14]. A popular, pre-revolutionary holiday that had been lost was St. Louis' Day, 25 August. St. Louis' Day was the official feast day of the Louis's of Bourbon France. At Brienne, the late summer *fête*, with its exhibitions, games and fireworks, was much anticipated by young Napoleon's classmates. He personally preferred to spend the free day quietly reading in his garden [7].

Of course, restoring St. Louis' Day was out of the question. But Napoleon's coming ascension to the throne immediately created two holidays. Then, as now, European monarchies celebrate, or at least recognize, the sovereign's birthday or feast day, and the coronation day. During the empire, Coronation Day (2 December 1804) was celebrated, particularly since the Battle of Austerlitz was on its first anniversary. The new emperor's feast day, however, posed some minor problems. He had no patron saint; and his own birthday (15

August) fell on the Feast of the Assumption of the Virgin, a major holy day not to be lightly usurped.

St. Napoleon neatly solved the hiccup, and then some. In one stroke, the Emperor obtained a patron saint, with a *fête* one day after his own birthday, and only 9 days before the fondly remembered St. Louis' Day. Eventually, the Fête of St. Napoleon, with celebrations indistinguishable from old St. Louis' Day, became a 2-day event. A decree of 1806 made it officially so.

Another subtle benefit (caution, dear reader, what follows is conjecture) is that St. Roch, whose fête is 16 August, was bumped off the calendar. It was on the steps of the Church of St. Roch that General Bonaparte fired the "whiff of grapeshot". A pivotal point in his career, but Napoleon would have been disinclined towards a yearly reminder that he had once fired on French citizens. Also, Napoleon found the present curè of the church, Claude Marie Marduel, an uncompromising fellow, and did not mind symbolically demoting him [15]. St. Roch was literally almost across the street from Napoleon's official residence, the Tuileries. Marduel's tenure as curè (1789-1833), the longest in St. Roch's history, encompassed a revolution, the Terror, an empire, a restoration and another revolution—all on the doorsteps of his church. So, Marduel must have been a tough man indeed.

Holidays or Holy Days

St. Napoleon became a fixture of the Empire. A masonic lodge was named for him. Biographical details—some allegedly from church scholars, some from no one knows where—came and went. Hymns were composed for him. His likeness, fashioned after the Emperor's, appeared on medallions and icons [6].

But throughout the Empire, "St. Napoleon" meant a 2-day summer *fête*, spanning 15-16 August. Of the twelve years (1802-1813) the *fête* was celebrated, Napoleon was in Paris for seven of them, was on campaign for three (1809, 1812 and 1813), and was twice with his army at Boulogne (1804 and 1805). His valet, Constant, describes [8] the 1804 *fête* at Boulogne, as "nothing more beautiful was ever seen, nor could be seen perhaps." It was the first distribution of the Legion of Honor among the army preparing for the invasion of England. Activity started at 6:00 AM, as 80,000 men moved toward the field where an elevated amphitheatre had been erected. At 10 o'clock in the morning:

> *"A salvo of artillery announced the departure of the Emperor. His Majesty started from his barrack, surrounded by more than 80 generals and 200 aides-de-camp; he was followed by his entire household. The Emperor...came at a gallop to the foot of the throne, amidst universal acclamations...His majesty ascended the throne, followed by his brothers and some of the great dignitaries. When he was seated, everybody took his place, and the distribution of crosses began in the following manner: an aide-de-camp of the Emperor called the designated soldiers, who came one by one...They were received by the arch-chancellor, who gave them their brevet. Two pages, stationed between the tripod and the Emperor, took the decoration from the helmet of Duguesclin and handed it to his Majesty, who attached it himself to the hero's breast. As he did so, more than 800 drummers beat a roll, and when the decorated soldier came down...1,200 musicians signalized the return of the legionary to his company."*

The ceremony continued for five hours, followed by joyous celebrations, fireworks and competitions, which continued into the next day.

In Paris, perhaps the most remembered *fête* was in 1807. The bloody Campaign of 1806-1807 ended successfully in June with the Battle of Friedland. On 27 July, the Emperor returned to Paris after 10 months absence. Amidst the homecoming celebrations of 15 August, Napoleon attended a mass at Notre Dame, and delivered a brief address [2]:

> *"Everything comes from God. He has granted me great victories. I come in the premiere capital of my Empire to render thanks to Providence for its gifts, and to recommend myself to your prayers and those of the clergy."*

His words may have been genuine; Eylau had been a close call.

In the power struggles between church and state, between Pope and Emperor, that arose soon after the signing of the Concordat, St. Napoleon's Day was used by both sides. The government watched

closely the sermons and proclamations issued from pulpits on that feast day. The pulpits were usually quite complimentary [4].
Occasionally, a reprimand was called for, as in Napoleon's dispatch of 19 September 1805 [3]:

> *"Let M. Robert, priest at Bourges, know that I am displeased with the very bad sermon which he preached on the 15th August."*

In 1813, with the Empire in its death throes, the annual celebration continued unabated, perhaps to bolster morale. A poster announcing the festivities in Rueil survives from this last St. Napoleon's Day, and hangs in the Bois Preau museum. A tolerable translation is:

FETE de St. NAPOLEON
Town of Rueil
Near Malmaison

The public is invited to a FETE de St. NAPOLEON, in Rueil near the Chateau Malmaison, which will take place 15-16 August 1813.
This Fête will take place at the "Quinconce des Maronniers", in front of Prince d'Essling Park.
It will consist of dances, games and other amusements. Illuminations will be placed around the Quinconce to the end of the street. Nothing will be overlooked to make the Fête enjoyable.
Assistance and protection will be provided for merchants in the area. Hazardous games are prohibited; all laws will be strictly observed.

How the Rueil *fête* came off is unknown, but the one in Paris had problems. Napoleon, in Germany preparing for what would be the Battle of Dresden, wrote his Grand Chamberlain [3]:

> *"I was much displeased to learn that matters were so badly managed on the 15th August that the Empress was detained for a considerable time listening to bad music, and that consequently the public were kept two hours waiting for the fireworks."*

The Death of a Saint

1813 saw the last *Fête* of St. Napoleon. The next day (17 August) hostilities resumed between France and the Allies, leading to Napoleon's decisive defeat at Leipzig in October. In April 1814 Napoleon abdicated, and never held power in August again (the Hundred Days spanned March to June). The saint was quickly forgotten, even by Bonapartists and Napoleon himself. His retinue celebrated his birthday; memoirs from Elba and St. Helena give several accounts of the doings each 15 August. No *fête* for St. Napoleon is mentioned. The casual dismissal of the saint is evident in a letter written 28 July 1814 [3] by Napoleon on Elba:

> *"As I am not yet sufficiently well lodged to give fêtes, I shall await the arrival of the Empress and the Princess Pauline whom I expect in the first days of September, to have fireworks."*

With the return of the Bourbons, the Fête of St. Louis was reinstated as the national holiday; and 16 August was returned to St. Roch. The Paris clergy chose 15 August 1814, to send Louis XVIII an address of praise that, as in the Ancien Regime, rang with *"Dieu et le Roi"* (God and the King) [13]. The Church, like so many others, was anxious to bury any traces of its cooperation with Napoleon, and withdrew all recognition of the saint. Even during the 2nd Empire, when invoking memories of the first Napoleon was state policy, St. Napoleon was hardly mentioned.

At St. Helena, the saint was mentioned rarely, and usually half in jest. Apparently, Napoleon never really took his patron saint very seriously. But it had been a useful instrument of policy.

The Name and the Man

How important is a person's name? For generations, conventional wisdom held that a name somehow curses or blesses its bearer. Hence, the restrictive naming traditions among many peoples. Study after study [5] shows no correlation between name and personality or achievement. Yet who among us has not had a friend who detested his name and blamed on it many misfortunes?

Napoleon subscribed to the conventional wisdom. His decree of 1803 protected newborns from their parents' folly. On St. Helena, he mused [10]:

> *Even my name, "Napoleon", which in Italy is uncommon, poetic and sonorous, contributed its share in the great circum*

stances of my life."

He did not elaborate. Was he correct? How different would those great circumstances have been had he, like his brothers, received a common name? Did he draw strength or luck from his name?

The power of a name is one issue, but changing a name is perhaps more serious. The exaggeration of Napoleon's name changes taps a deep mistrust. To the end of his days, his opponents called him "Buonaparte". Entertainers and artists excepted, we tend to be wary of persons who alter their names. In recent history, at least two presidential candidates and a heavyweight champion learned the consequences of that mistrust.[6] Changes of name are often associated with villains. Though Hitler only modernized the spelling of his given name, he was widely taunted as "Adolph Schicklgruber".[7] Ioseb Dzhugashvili certainly did change his name to Josef Stalin. An easy way to link Napoleon with them is to cast a similar accusation at him. But such a charge is simply unfounded.

Villains can sour a name, but heroes can enoble theirs. In ancient Macedonia, a most common male name was "Alexandros" [12]. Alexandros III—to us, Alexander the Great—infused that ordinary name with qualities it still holds today. The same is true of "Caesar". In a particularly bitter passage from Shakespeare, Cassius pulls Brutus aside and whispers:

"Brutus" and "Caesar"—what should be in that "Caesar"?
Why should that name be sounded more than your's?
Write them together, your's is as fair a name.
Sound them, it doth become the mouth as well.
Weigh them, it is as heavy. Conjure with them—
"Brutus" will start a spirit as soon as "Caesar"!
Now, in the name of all the gods at once,
Upon what meat did this our "Caesar" feed
That he has grown so great?

The greatness comes not from the name, but from the man himself.

The Emperor's tomb in the Invalides bears no name. There, amidst the enshrined tributes to his military and civil achievements, "Napoleon", whatever spirits it conjures, is hardly missed.

References

1. Aronson, Theo; "Napoleon & Josephine - A Love Story", John Murrary, Ltd., 1990.
2. Barnett, Corelli; "Bonaparte", Hill & Wang, 1978.
3. Bingham, D. A., "Letters & Dispatches of the 1st Napoleon", 1884, Chapman & Hall, 3 Volumes.
4. Bourrienne, Louis A. F. de, "Memoirs of Napoleon Bonaparte", 1891, Charles Scribner's Sons, 4 Volumes. On page 208 of volume 3, a particularly subservient sermon is quoted: "God chose Napoleon for his representative on Earth..." Bourrienne is, of c course not to be trusted; but more reputable sources also comment on Napoleon's domination of the Church of France.
5. Browder, Sue, "The New Age Baby Name Book", Warner Books 1987.
6. Carlson, John (editor), "The Saints - A Concise Biographical Dictionary", New York, Guild Press, 1957
7. Carrington, Dorothy, "Napoleon & His Parents - On the Threshold of History", Dutton, 1990. This book is an outstanding achievement. This article has drawn from it many times.
8. Constant, Louis Wairy, "Memoirs of Constant on the Private Life of Napoleon", translated by E. G. Martin, The Century Company, 1907, 4 Volumes.
9. Cronin, Vincent; "Napoleon", Penguin Books, 1983
10. Las Cases, Count de, "Memoirs of the Life, Exile and Conversations of the Emperor Napoleon", 1855, Redfield, 4 volumes.
11. O'Meara, Barry E.; "Napoleon in Exile or A Voice from St. Helena", W.J. Widdleton, 1879, 2 volumes. Napoleon made this statement on 29 September 1817.
12. Renault, Mary; "The Alexander Trilogy", Penguin Books, 1984.
13. Stendhal, "A Life of Napoleon", Rodale Press, 1956.
14. Stevenson, Seth William, "Journal of a Tour through Part of France, Flanders & Holland including a Visit to Paris, and a Walk Over the Field of Waterloo Made in the Summer of 1816", Norfolk Chronicle Press, 1817. This book's appendix includes passages from Stevenson's dairy of 1802. Regarding Bastille Day, he notes that "this anniversary brings with it ideas for which the Revolu-

tion-sick Parisians have lost all relish. They like the Fête, but care little for the occasion."
15. Thompson, J. M., "Napoleon Bonaparte", Basil Blackwell, Ltd., 1952.
16. Wall St. Journal, "In France, the Name You Give Your Child May Not Last Long", 6 June 1987, New York, page 1.

Footnotes
1. Numbers in brackets, [ ], refer to references listed at the end of the text. Superscripts refer to footnotes.
2. They are quite numerous, and include Neopoli, Neopolis, Napoli (Naples), Napolion, Neapoleone, Napoleone, Nabulio, Nebulion.
3. To continue the ironies—Napoleon was responsible for putting the Guelphs and Ghibellines forever to rest: 1) Rather than cede the purely ceremonial title of Holy Roman Emperor to his conqueror and future son-in-law, Francis II of Austria dissolved it in 1806; 2) The Catholic monarchs of Europe cringed in horror at Napoleon's blunt treatment of the Pope, but his example soon led to the end of the Pope's temporal powers.
4. Joseph's given name was "Guiseppe Napoleone", which on his baptismal certificate, written in Latin, is "Ioseph Nabulion"
5. In Greek, something akin to "lion of the woods" can be wrung from "Napoleon". But this, a tortured Greek translation of the French form of a Latinized Greek word, is meaningless.
6. Gary Hart (Hartpenz), Pete (Pierre) Dupont and Muhammad Ali (Cassius Clay)
7. Hitler's father, Alois, was born illegitimately in 1837 and used his mother's name "Schicklgruber". Alois adopted "Hitler" long before his son's birth, and "Hitler", with minor spelling variations, was the only family name the son ever knew. At the beginning of his political career, his opponents taunted Hitler with his father's murky past and the easily-parodied name. "Schicklgruber" dogged Hitler for the rest of his life.

Frank K. Dello Stritto was born in New Jersey in 1950. He received his bachelor's in physics, and his master's and Ph.D. in ocean engineering from Stevens Institute of Technology. Since 1977, he has worked for Mobil Research and Development Corporation in a variety of locations. He now lives in Bensalem, PA. Frank has had a life-long interest in Napoleon, which blossomed while he was living in Europe in 1982. His main interest is the personal life of the Emperor, and his relationships with his friends and his family.

Napoleon- An Operational Genius But a Strategic Failure

By Professor Steven Ross, U.S. Naval War College, Newport, R.I.

French military operations during the American Revolutionary War were limited. The major battle fought by the French Expeditionary Corps was the siege of Yorktown, a formal almost mathematical process. The French did carefully plan their march to Virginia with their American ally and effectively coordinated the land campaign with the navy in order to isolate the British force and prevent reinforcements from reaching the beseiged garrison. The monarchy emerged victorious from its limited war, but less than a decade later contributed to its own destruction by encouraging the nation to go to war in Europe in the hope that foreign armies would crush the Revolution and restore royal authority. The emotions unleashed by the conflict and growing popular suspicion of Louis XVI led to the popular uprisings of August 1792, the destruction of the monarchy, and to the king's arrest, trial, and execution.

By the fall of 1793, the new Republic, fighting alone against the First Coalition, had established its authority throughout most of France, mobilzed the nation's resources, and identified the most dangerous threats to the state's security and survival. Strategically the government intended to mount its major operations on the northern front since the most immediate threat to Paris emanated from Anglo-Austrian forces operating in Belgium and northern France. The Committee of Public Safety also felt that the Republic had to crush the internal forces of counterrevolution. The Committee instructed its generals to attack vigorously and continually, to ignore geographic objectives, and to focus their efforts on the destruction of the enemy field armies. The Committee did not expect a single decisive victory to decide the course of the campaign. Rather, the government presumed that constant attacks would wear down British and Austrian strength, exhaust their reserves, and enable Republican forces to shatter them at some point. Finally, the Committee ordered commanders to follow up any victory with a relentless pursuit. The Committee also announced that France had no intentions of interfering in the internal affairs of other states, a move designed not only to assure foreign governments that the Republic was not attempting to overturn the status quo of the entire Continent but also to reassure the French public that the government's sole concern was national survival.

The Republic thus pursued a strategy of attrition designed to weaken hostile forces until they could no longer resist effectively. Although not entirely successful in 1793, the armies of the Republic did halt the forces of the Coalition in the north, defeated counterrevolutionary forces in the interior, and contained other coalition operations on the southern and eastern frontiers.

In preparing the campaign of 1794, the Committee of Public Safety presumed that the overall strategic situation remained essentially the same as in the previous year. England and Austria remained the most dedicated foes of the Republic, and their armies posed the most direct threat to Paris. Prussia, Spain, and the lesser Coalition members might be convinced to leave the war by diplomatic means. Counterrevolutionary forces, though not completely destroyed, posed no immediate threat, and victory against the Coalition would probably prevent a resurgance of insurrection. The Committee, therefore, reinforced the armies on the northern frontier and ordered them to meet and halt the forthcoming Coalition offensive and then to launch a major series of assaults along a line running from Flanders to the Sambre River. The armies were to stand on the defensive in the center and deliver their blows on the flanks in order to make it difficult for the Coalition to shift reserves to threatened areas, attenuate Allied forces, and finally to break the enemy cordon.

In the spring of 1794, the Coalition forces struck first, but on May 17, the Army of the North halted their advance. On the Sambre the force that was soon to become the famous Army of the Sambre-Meuse crossed the river on May 20. Hurled back, the French attacked again on May 26. Defeated a second time the French returned to the assault and crossed the river yet again on May 29 only to driven back on June 3. Meanwhile, the Army of the North began to advance on Ypres. Halted on June 10, the army struck again three days later but was unable to take the city. A third attack on June 17 was successful, and the Army of the North drove the Allies from Ypres. The Army of the Sambre-Meuse returned to the attack on June 12 when it crossed the river and held a bridgehead until the 16th. On June 18, the French attacked again and finally succeeded in securing a firm lodgement on the Austrian side of the river. On June 26, the French met and defeated a smaller Austrian force that was attempting to relieve the garrison at Charleroi. The Battle of Fleurus succeeded in finally dislocating the entire Allied position in Belgium.

As the Allies retreated the French mounted a relentless pursuit. The Army of the North moved through Belgium towards the Netherlands, and the Sambre-Meuse Army advanced into Belgium and then swung east in order to advance into the Rhineland. On July 17, the Sambre-Meuse entered Kaiserslautern, and ten days later the Army of the North occupied Antwerp.

Trier fell on August 9, and by the turn of the year, the Army of the North was pushing rapidly into the Netherlands against disintegrating opposition.

Substantial numbers, an effective tactical system. a very simple logistics system, and well motivated patriotic troops enabled the armies of the Republic to meet the professional forces of Old Regime Europe on at least equal terms. The ability of a Republican army to attack again and again, to suffer defeat after defeat, and to persevere until rewarded with victory was unique in modern European warfare. Old Regime armies typically fought one or two major battles per campaigning season and if victorious were rarely able to launch an effective pursuit. The armies of the Republic were able to offer numerous battles and in the wake of victory to mount a pursuit that enabled commanders to turn a tactical victory into a strategic triumph. The Republican strategy of attrition did not guarantee victory, and French armies suffered numerous defeats. Nonetheless, the strategy of attrition did provide French decision makers with a range of military options not hitherto available to the nation's leaders.

Napoleon moved beyond the strategy of attrition to a strategy of annihilation. He did so by eliminating flaws in the Republican tactical system, perfecting tactical and operational methods, and adding to them the quality of his own unique genius. Initially, Napoleon employed the attrition style of warfare. His Italian Campaign of 1796 and 1797 did, of course, involve a dazzling display of rapid maneuver, but victory was a result of a series of engagements involving a small force of 25 to 30,000 men. No single battle was decisive, but the cumulative effect of Napoleon's small victories was to exhaust the Austrians who were also fighting French forces in southern Germany, force them out of Northern Italy, and compel them to sue for peace.

The Marengo Campaign of 1800 hinted at Bonaparte's desired approach to operations and strategy. He focused Austrian efforts against the French garrison at Genoa and personally led the Army of Reserve through Switzerland to emerge in the Austrian rear. Cut off from escape and pinned against the Ligurian coast, the Austrians would be destroyed in a single campaign. Far from being a smashing triumph culminating in the destruction of the enemy force, Marengo was almost a resounding defeat for Napoleon. On the field of battle Napoleon was rescued from disaster only by the bravery and intelligent judgement of one of his subordinates. Fortunately for Napoleon, the subordinate was killed in the engagement, and he was able to write the bulletin describing the battle. Naturally, he reported that everything went according to plan thereby enhancing his reputation in France. Despite its inadequacies, the Marengo Campaign was, nevertheless, an early Napoleonic attempt to execute a strategy of annihilation.

The Amiens peace and the absence of hostilities on the Continent until 1805 gave Napoleon the opportunity to enhance the army's capabilities by rigorous training. In the camps along the Channel coast, the army exercised daily. The weekly schedule involved drill at all levels of organization, and days were assigned for corps level evolutions as well as for grand reviews where several corps maneuvered in front of the Emperor. Veterans of previous campaigns, about

50 per cent of the army's strength, sharpened their skills, and new recruits received the benefit of careful instruction by experienced NCO's and junior officers. Throughout French garrisons, inspector generals examined battalion and company level officers on their knowledge of drill regulations, and weekly meetings of iunior officers and NCO's to discuss tactics sharpened individual understanding of the army's doctrine.

Napoleon's 1805 campaign - the march to the Danube, the encirclement at Ulm, the thrust into Bohemia, and the Battle of Austerlitz-demonstrated just how effective the French army under the Emperor's inspired leadership had become. A single campaign culminating in one major battle sufficed to dislocate the Third Coalition and force Austria to sue for peace. The Prussian Campaign of 1806 was even more decisive, for in little more than a month Napoleon not only crushed his enemy's army but also eliminated Prussia's ability to offer further resistance. At the end of the campaign Napoleon could in fact have obliterated the Prussian kingdom.

In the fall of 1806 Prussia, goaded into action by Napoleon's cavalier treatment of Berlin's interests and sovereignty, declared war on France. After occupying Saxony, the Prussian army, 171,000 men strong, intended to march due west towards the Rhine. The Prussians assumed that the Grand Army, garrisoned in Bavaria, would hasten north to defend the Empire's eastern border. The concentrated Prussian force would encounter the scattered French corps and defeat them in detail. Napoleon, of course, had no intention of simply responding to his enemy's strategic initiatives. Rather, he intended to impose his will opon them and mount a campaign that would not just defeat the Prussians but destroy them completely.

Napoleon ordered the Grand Army to advance northeast from Bavaria into Saxony. The army moved in the famous *battalion carré* with each corps moving by seperate roads while remaining within supporting distance of each other. If a corps encountered the main Prussian force, it would be able to resist alone for 24 hours while the other corps advanced to its assistance. Napoleon's maneuver was designed to outflank the Prussian field army, threaten their supply bases, place the French between the field army and Berlin and other garrisons, and disorient and confuse the Prussian high command. Napoleon intended to compel the Prussians to fight on his terms and the deep rapid drive into Saxony had the desired effect.

The Grand Army began to advance on October 8. The Prussians were stunned by the audacity of the French advance. They dropped all thoughts of moving west, and within five days of the initial French strike. the Prussian army attempted to organize a hasty retreat to the east. The Prussians, however, reacted too late, and on October 14, 1806, Napoleon with 96,000 men caught and crushed the Prussian rear guard at the Battle of Jena. On the same day, Davout's IIIrd Corps, 26,000 men strong, encountered and routed the 63,000 troops of the Prussian main army at the Battle of Auerstadt. The ability of the outnumbered French corps to defeat a much larger force indicates the level of ascendency that the French had achieved at all levels of war.

After his dual triumphs, the Emperor conducted a devastating pursuit. French troops entered Berlin on October 25 and reached the Baltic Sea four days later. By November 5, leading elements of the Grand Army stood on the Elbe. The rapid exploitation of victory prevented the Prussians from rallying for another stand and turned the defeat of the army into an utter catastrophy for the state. Towns and cities closed their gates to the fleeing Prussian forces, and inhabitants of Berlin jeered Prussian officers as the French led them through the city on the way to captivity. In 33 days the Grand Army marched from Bavaria to the Baltic and in the process of a single campaign destroyed completely one of Europe's largest and best trained armies. Moreover, Napoleon had not only destroyed the Prussian army but also held the very existence of the state and the Hohenzollern dynasty at his mercy. With a stroke of the pen he could have proclaimed the abolition of serfdom and with it the end of the monarchy. Alternatively he could have partitioned Prussia, rewarding his German allies with portions of the Hohenzollern kingdom.

Warfare had taken on a new dimension. Napoleon had demonstrated his ability not just to defeat but to annihilate an opponent's military and political capabilities to resist his will, and he achieved his goal in the course of a single devastating and decisive campaign. Carl von Clausewitz, the great Prussian theorist of war, participated in the disaster of 1806 and later wrote that if the Revolution unleashed the energies of an entire people, Napoleon harnessed these energies to raise war to its absolute form.,

Yet on a higher level, the 1806 campaign was oddly inconclusive. Prussia survived the debacle and later reformed the state's political and military institutions in order to recover its great power status. Wars continued, and the power balance finally turned against the Emperor. Napoleon achieved about as much as any man had accomplished with armed force, yet his failures at the higher levels of strategy deprived his military triumphs of any long term political or strategic value.

Within France Napoleon dominated all aspects of government in a regime that was centralized far beyond the wildest dreams of even the most powerful French kings. The church, the schools, and the press obediently executed the Emperor's bidding while an extensive network of local officials and police spies kept the government informed about the state of public opinion. No factions or cliques could challenge the Emperor or thwart his will. Nor was he at the mercy of shifting electoral majorities. Administratively and bureaucratically Napoleon had virtually a free hand to create and control French policy and strategy, yet he was singularly inept at identifying both short and long term threats to his Empire.

Adaptation to a Changing Strategic Environment

Whereas the monarchy and the Republic were aware of actual and potential threats and the need to respond to them with diplomatic and political as well as military means, Napoleon persisted in relying upon his legions and his own formidable command abilities to resolve all of his strategic dilemas.

The monarchy never went to war without alllies, and the Republic was also aware of the need and value of alliances. In 1796, France concluded a formal pact with Bourbon Spain. The Republic also employed diplomacy to reduce the number of its enemies. In 1795 France signed a peace treaty with Prussia and in 1796 - 1797 undertook direct peace negotiations with Great Britain. Since the Republic was born and lived in a perpetual state of war, the government had little opportunity to contemplate long term threats to its security. Both the

Committee of Public Safety and the Directory, however, realized that England and Austria were their most dangerous foes and constantly tried to force both powers to come to terms with France.

Napoleon never seems to have felt the need to employ diplomacy as an integral part of his strategy or to make concessions to keep potential foes from joining the enemy camp. In the late summer of 1813, for example, he faced a potentially disasterous situation as for the first time during the entire Revolutionary and Napoleonic period all of Europe's great powers were simultaneously at war with France. Napoleon had rebuilt his army after the debacle of the Russian campaign and deployed as many as half a million troops in Germany. Many of his soldiers, however, lacked sufficient training while many veterans were tied down in isolated and beseiged garrisons in north and eastern Germany. The regiments were not of the same quality as the Grand Army formations of 1805 - 1807. He was seriously short of cavalry and outnumbered by the forces of the Coalition. Moreover, in Spain, substantial manpower was continuing to wage a losing war against British, Spanish, and Portugese forces.

Still, the strategic situation was not completely hopeless. There were serious rifts within the hostile coalition. Austria was by no means anxious to see Napoleon completely defeated. Tied to France by the 1810 marriage alliance and fearful of Russian and Prussian ambitions in east and central Europe, Vienna would have been quite willing to maintain a large powerful French Empire as a counterweight to its northern and eastern neighbors. Moreover, all of the eastern powers were frankly awed and apprehensive at the prospect of having to face Napoleon on the field of battle.

A French diplomatic offensive while the Grand Army was still largely intact might well have produced positive results. Even after the defeat at Leipzig, Napoleon retained the option of using the Austrian inspired Frankfurt Proposals as a basis for negotiation. Throughout the campaign of 1814, Napoleon continued to reject peace proposals that would have left much of his power and much of his Empire intact. Limited wars were, however, never a part of Napoleon's calculations. He was unwilling to settle for half or even three quarters of a loaf and was determined to reverse his bleak political and strategic situation by war. He believed until the end that he could score another decisive victory and annihilate his opposition. He ignored the larger aspects of strategic dilema and never saw that the combination of British gold and allied manpower had irrevocably altered the balance of forces. Napoleon's almost exclusive reliance on the military option and the obsessive search for decisive battles and campaigns virtually foreclosed other avenues of approach leaving him unable to adjust to changes in the operational and strategic environment.

The Strategic Product

The Monarchy, the Republic, and the Empire had to respond to changes in the strategic environment. The crown reacted effectively in the realm of foreign affairs and made significant efforts to improve the state's military capabilities. The monarchy, however, failed to devise means to tap the nation's fiscal resources, and financial problems coupled with the king's political ineptitude contributed to the coming of the Revolution. In trying to use a war to resolve its domestic problems the crown sealed its doom. The Republic also responded and adapted to the external environment but fell victim to its inability to establish a general consensus concerning the political future of the state. By contrast Napoleon had few threatening domestic problems. The vast majority of Frenchmen accepted him as the legitimate ruler of France. His failures lay in the realm of foreign policy and strategy where his refusal to alter or modify his reliance on armed force made him inflexible and unable to meet escalating challenges.

Response to Change

A fiscal crisis caused in large measure by the inability to pay for previous wars forced the crown to summon the Estates General. As the revolution of the Third Estate unfolded Louis XVI had to make a crucial choice. He could either take the leadership of the reform movement sacrificing some of his power but enhancing the popularity and security of the ruling house or resist change and take the path of counterrevolution. Bourbon monarchs in the past had sided with the lower orders, but Louis chose the path of resistance. Consequently, he accepted political changes only under pressure. His flight to Varennes in 1791 and the pitiful failure to spark a counterrevolution further undermined his already fragile popularity and authority. In desperation Louis supported the drift towards war in the hope that foreign troops would accomplish what he had been unable to achieve with his own resources - the destruction of the revolution. The emotions unleashed by the conflict and the growing suspicion of the king's real motives led ultimately to the complete destruction of the monarchy. Louis failed to win the support of the French people, and his inability to rally popular backing led to his doom.

Republican governments also faced the problem of dealing with public opinion. In 1792 Danton rallied the people of Paris and virtually forced the Assembly to agree to defend the city against the advancing Prussian army. The Committee of Public Safety found that in strategic decision making and economic mobilization public opinion was a critical factor. The Committee ordered offensives in the fall of 1793 in part because the Parisian populace demanded a vigorous and victorious prosecution of the war. A major element in the introduction of price controls was popular demands for stable prices for bread and other basic necessities of life. A total war in a democratic state requires above all else broad public support, and the Committee of Public Safety responded successfully to this fundamental need.

War weariness, the persistance of royalist and Jacobin sentiment. and serious economic problems presented insurmountable problems for the Directory. The Directory was quite proficient in diplomatic and strategic affairs, but because of its narrow base of political support, the regime could never win acceptance as the legitimate government of France from a majority of the politically active French people. The government, therefore had constant recourse to the use of force to repress opposition from both the left and the right. Insurrections were crushed in the streets, and adverse election results were undone by army backed purges. Despite victory in foreign wars, the Robespierrist Committee of Public Safety and the Directory failed to create a domestic political consensus, and both governments were destroyed. Having mobilized the populace and led the nation in war, French governments were unable to establish their domestic legitimacy, and success in war was undone by failure at home.

As Consul and as Emperor, Napoleon did gain general acceptance by the French public. Many revered him, and others regarded him as an acceptable alternative to the excesses of revolution and as a guardian against the return of the old order. An intuitive expert at propaganda, he maintained public support almost to the end of his reign. His failure, unlike previous governments, did not lay in the realm of domestic affairs but in foreign policy and strategy. His commitment to a policy of expansion without rational limits pursued by a strategy of annihilation never changed. His failure to recognize that the power balance had shifted, that his enemies were stronger, and that a strategy of annihilation in a single campaign was no longer feasible doomed him to defeat. His persistence in seeking another Austerlitz or a second Jena is perhaps not surprising given the startling triumphs that Napoleon had in fact achieved. Always dangerous in battle, Napoleon, even when cornered, could and did lash out unexpectedly and inflict stinging defeats on his enemies. Nevertheless, his refusal to accept the fact that his strategic environment had changed spelt doom for his Empire. If the failure to respond effectively to the imperatives of domestic politics contributed to the destruction of the monarchy and the Republic, the failure to deal with the external environment destroyed the Empire.

Measures of Success and Failure

The monarchy and the Republic were on the whole successful in devising and executing strategy against external enemies. The government of Louis XVI emerged victorious from its only major war. The Republic, faced with catastrophe, mobilized the nation's human and material resources and successfully defended the national territory. The Republic defeated two great power coalitions and came close to achieving international recognition, and a victorious peace. In November, 1799, Napoleon seized control of a government that had already turned the tide of battle in a major multi-front conflict and was on the path to a successful conclusion of the war. The Amiens Treaty, concluded by Napoleon, fulfilled the goals of the Republic which, despite its failure to establish a domestic political consensus, had been reasonably successful in defining national obiectives and devising appropriate strategies to achieve them.

Napoleon's genius at the operational level of war and his ability to conduct a strategy of annihilation was not linked to a policy that had sensible national objectives. To treat great but finite power as infinite led ultimately to an overextension of French resources and to disaster. Throughout his career as Consul and Emperor, Napoleon had non-military options which he could have employed to stabilize his regime, but his restless and relentless drive for constant expansion precluded their use. The greatest general of his age, triumphant on battlefields from Italy to Moscow, failed because he ignored broader strategic realities, and his legacy to future generations was and remains ambiguous.

The Napoleonic Strategic Legacy

After 1815, soldiers and scholars naturally were drawn to the study of the Emperor's campaigns both for their inherent interest and excitement and for the operational and tactical lessons they contained. Baron Jomini, a veteran of the Napoleonic Wars, quickly emerged as the leading interpreter of the Napoleonic experience. He attempted to reduce the Napoleonic art of war to a science which officers could study and imitate. He formulated a set of clear concise operational principles which commanders could employ to wage campaigns of Napoleonic proportions. To those confounded and frightened by Napoleon's genius on the field of battle, Jomini provided reassurance. Napoleon, according to Jomini, was indeed unique, but his methods were subject to rational analysis and imitation. Others could learn to understand the Emperor's methods and could apply them to their own situations. To Jomini, the operational art of war was the proper sphere of the commander. Politics, diplomacy, and economic factors were important, but they were the business of the political leadershlp. The professional soldier should confine his role to executing the orders of his political masters and to devoting his efforts to the planning and waging of campaigns and battles.

Carl von Clausewitz, another veteran of the Napoleonic Wars, argued that in war, intangibles - morale, fear, friction, and genius - play a crucial role. More critically, Clausewitz felt that war was not an isolated activity to be conducted by professionals in isolation from the broader concerns of the nation. War, Clausewitz believed, was a political instrument, and although it had its own grammer it did not have its own logic. War was one element in a much broader context of the nation's strategy. Thus, to argue that a government should simply inform the general of the state's objectives and then permit the general to conduct operations with no further reference to the national goals was an absurdity. War was permeated by political considerations at all levels, and if commanders ignored the broader aspects of strategy, the nation would run grave risks. Jomini's emphasis on the operational rather than the strategic aspects of war, however, became the dominant view. Military men found the notion that war was indeed an isolated autonomus act simpler and more conducive to their professional *raison d'etre* than the more complex demands that Clausewitz would place upon them.

Generations of military leaders came to assume that the proper sphere for professional study and attention was the realm of tactics and operations. They willingly relinquished broader strategic considerations to the political leadership in return for autonomy in the conduct of operations. German and later other military professionals came to view Clausewitz as the advocate of the massive battle of annihilation, and many German generals stated with some perverse pride that the larger import of Clausewitz's work went largely ignored in their military education. Officers studied the campaigns of Frederick the Great, Hannibal, and Napoleon; the theoretical views of Clausewitz were dismissed as being relevant only to professors.

Throughout the 19th and 20th Centuries, studies on Napoleon's tactics and operational art proliferated, and they served to confirm the implicit belief of professional soldiers that operational considerations were indeed a proper substitute for an examination of the complexities of strategy. The notion that commanders need not be concerned about public opinion, diplomacy, coalition warfare, or the economic aspects of defense, other than the struggle for a larger share of the national budget still persists, and many seem to have forgotten one of the most important lessons to be derived from the Napoleonic experience - no amount of operational and tactical brilliance can offset gross political and strategic incompetence.

* * *

Professor Steven Ross earned his doctoral degree in military history at Princeton University. He has taught at the Naval War College in Newport, R.I. since 1973. He is the author of eight books and 40 articles dealing with military affairs.

Family, Francs, and Frontiers
by Timothy Kirkpatrick, Swansea, IL

I have been invited to speak to you on two of my favorite topics, passions if you will, Napoleonic history and numismatics, or the lore and history of coins. Pictured is a medallion from the David Markham collection featuring Napoleon. Napoleon obviously had a major impact on European politics. one of the most powerful effects of a state is the coining and regulation of money. Napoleon and the changes of the Revolutionary period, also left a mark on the money of the period.

Pictured here on a silver ecu is Louis XVI in happier days. The coin carries the motto "King by the Grace of God", with the Royal Bourbon *fleur-de-lis*.

Here we have an early Revoultionary period coin, a denier. France is now a constitutional monarchy, and here we see Louis King of France with the motto "the rule of law". Here is a six livres from the Revolutionary period, dated 1793. This is a very interesting piece as Louis had been deposed in September 1792 and France was now a Republic. Further, Louis was executed in January 1793. So the mint masters were a little late with this design. Note on the obverse we have a winged figure of Liberty writing the new Constitution of France. Louis was succeeded by the Directory. Under the law of 1795 the money was changed and the new system of francs and centimes was instituted. Also, between 1792 and 1795, the Revolutionary government began issuing paper assignats. These paper notes based their value on the value of church lands and noble landed estates confiscated by the government. When first issued these notes carried a premium on the market of 95 francs paper for 100 francs silver. The government printed massive amounts of the paper, in order to finance the war effort. Inflation resulted and by 1796 the now very unpopular asignats, 20 billion, were worth a nominal 200 million. The government had ruined the money.

Then came this fellow Napoleon, and the coup of Brumaire, and the formation of the Consulate. Napoleon continued the ban on the issuing of paper money imposed by his predecessors, and the minting of gold coins resumed. Here is a medallion featuring the three new Consuls, a medallion of General Bounoparte, and a gold 20 franc from the Consulate period dated L'AN12. Note the new legend "*Republique Francaise.*"

As the Consulate evolved into the Empire, the coins also changed. The coins sported a combination of the bust of the Consul and the legend "*Republique Francaise,*" a bust of Empereur Napoleon and the legend "*Republique Francaise,*" and finally a bust of Empereur Napoleon and the legend "*Empire Francaise.*". Also, after the coronation in 1804, the year XIII, Julian dating resumed with 1806 being the first date to appear on the coins. Here is an 1808 silver one franc with *Napoleon Empereur,* still bearing the legend "*Republique Francaise.*" This slide shows the final evolution of Empire coinage, an 1812 5 franc. Here is an 1810 copper 10 centime, with the rather unique incuse minting style, the letters are stamped into the planchet, with just the monogram "N" and a crown as the obverse design.

As a political leader Napoleon was also featured as the King of Italy on coins from that state. Here is a lovely copper three centissimi with a bust of a young Napoleon, with the Iron Crown of Italy on the reverse. Here is a rather nice coat of arms for the King of Italy on a silver 5 lire. Napoleon never had his coat of arms put on French coins in order not to upset Republican sensibilities. Here is a gold 20 lire, which had the same gold content as French gold 20 Francs .

Now all of this talk about coin designs and franc and lire is nice, but what does it mean to this fellow? A private in the Imperial Guard made 34.80 francs a month; a private in the regular line infantry made only 1/4 that amount, or 9 francs a month. After serving ten years in the ranks he was entitled to an extra franc a month! A senior NCO earned 24 francs a month. A second lieutenant made 90 francs a month, and a General of Division made 1,250 francs a month. A Marshal made a base salary of 3,333 francs a month, or 39,000 francs a year.

At this time a common day laborer made a franc a day, a skilled laborer, such as a locksmith, or an artisan made 4-5 francs a day. The prefect of Paris made 30,000 francs a year, a prefect in an outlaying province made as little as 8,000 francs a year.

The Legion of Honor was founded with a grant of 200,000 francs. In the beginning recipients could be awarded the title of Duke with a grant of 200,000 francs and land worth 20,000 francs, down to the lowest rank of Knight, with a grant of 3,000 francs. Now if you were a private in the infantry making 30 centimes a day, the possibility of winning the immense sum of 3,000 francs for valor must have been quite an incentive. That's equal to almost 20 years salary for that man!

Other interesting figures include 80 million francs for the sale of the Louisiana territories to the U.S.; that works out to 5.33 francs to the dollar for the $15 million the U.S. paid, which isn't much different from today's exchange rate. It was mentioned earlier that a conscript could buy his way out of the draft. That he could, but for 2,000 francs, or almost two year's salary for the average working man. Further the local gendarmes were awarded 12 francs for capturing a deserter or draft dodger. For 1,000 francs you could get a license signed by Napoleon to be a privateer under the flag of France.

Captain Coignet of the Imperial Guard states in his memoirs that he had his life savings on him during the Russian campaign, 700 francs.

On the retreat from Moscow he was trading 25 francs in silver for 20 francs in gold, in order to reduce the weight he was carrying. Think of that, a Captain in the Imperial Guard, a prestigious person and mid-ranking officer, and his life savings was just 700 francs. A 20 franc piece was 1/2 a month's wages for the average working man perhaps equivalent to a $500 bill in our day.

As Napoleon advanced across Europe and placed relatives on newly created thrones, they also began appearing on the coins of those states. Here is Joseph, King of Spain on a 4 reales. Joseph did not change the denominations or designs of the coins, perhaps in an effort to placate Spanish nationalism. He did add a small French Imperial eagle onto the coat of arms of Castille. Joseph had appeared earlier as the King of Naples, on the coins of that state. Here is Jerome, King of Westphalia. Jerome issued coins in both the German thaler and pfenig, and he issued coins in common with the French centimes and francs, again with the same silver and gold content as their French counterparts. This was an effort by Napoleon to encourage trade within the Empire. Here is a nice copper piece with "HN" for Hieronymous Napoleon, or Jerome. Here is the reverse with incuse stamping of the design. Here is a 5 franchii from the Principality of Lucca with Napoleon's sister Elisa and her husband Felix the hussar. Other members of the family who appeared on coins from the period also include Murat on coins from the Grand Duchy of Berg, and later as King of Naples, and Louis as King of Holland.

The Marshals also left their mark on the coinage of the period. Here is an 1808 schilling from the Duchy of Danzig, featuring the coat of arms of Marshal Lefevbre. He had been awarded his Marshal's baton and the Duchy of Danzig for his conduct while in charge of the seige of Danzig. Marshal Berthier, chief of staff, was awarded tbe Duchy of Neuchatel in Switzerland for his services to the Empereur, and his coat of arms appears on coins from that canton. He also received 300,000 francs when awarded his Marshal's baton; Marshal Ney received 800,000 francs.

A couple of new countries also modified their coinage; here is a 10 grozsy from the Grand Duchy of Warsaw, a state created by Napoleon. It featured the coat of arms of the King of Saxony, the nominal ruler of that state. Here is a copper 1 kreuzer from the Confederation of the Rhine, an association of allied German states.

Here are some examples of coins from some of Napoleon's opponents. Here is a Prussian 1/6 thaler with Frederick William II; a copper coin from Austria with Francis I. Note that this coin was minted after Austria's defeat in 1805, and the distablishment of the Holy Roman Empire. Prior to that he was Francis II. Here is a picture of some of that English gold with George III on a 1/3 gold Guinea of 1804. Booing is permitted.

What did the Empire mean in income for France? Italy was worth

30 million francs annually. Austria paid 75 million francs after her defeat in 1805, and another 164 million after her defeat in 1809. Prussia paid almost 500 million francs between 1807-1812.

Coins were even affected by the Hundred Days and the first abdication. Here is a 1815 copper decime with an "L" for Louis XVIII, reverse with the Royal fleuer. Here is a silver 5 franc with Louis XVIII. Louis did not change the monetary system, and he kept the francs and their silver content the same.

Here is a gold 20 franc with Napoleon dated 1815, from the Hundred Days. The mint masters, being good government bureaucrats, did not destroy the old coin dies when Louis gained the throne. They put them up on a shelf, and when Napoleon regained the throne in 1815 they dusted the dies off and began minting new 20 francs with Napoleon on them. This coin definitely was minted between March and June 1815. Silver 2 and 5 franc pieces were also minted during the Hundred Days. Here is a copper medallion, a form of propaganda all through this period, struck at the time showing the return of the Imperial Eagle from Elba.

The Empereur's legend also followed him to St. Helena. Here is a copper 1/2 penny from the East India Company at St. Helena, dated 1821, the year of Napoleon's death.

Unfortunately all good things must come to an end, and so must this talk. You can trace the political developments of Revolutionary and Napoleonic Europe through its coins. These are authentic artifacts from those times that have literally passed through their hands into ours. Just imagine whose pockets they traveled in, what battlefields they were on, perhaps even a gold 20 franc handed out by Napoleon himself to some soldier at attention, as he used to do. These coins are mini-time machines. Hold one in your hand and you touch the face of history.

• • •

Tim was born and raised in Minneapolis, Minnesota, and graduated from the University of Minnesota in 1973. He has had a life long love for history, with a strong concentration on military history, and numismatics. He has combined both these fields with his small coin business featuring coins of the Napoleonic era. Tim was an early member of the NSA, and has attended four of the annual conventions, speaking at two of them. He has worked for the federal government for 19 years, 18 of them in the Washington D.C. area. Tim, with his wife Claire and their three children, currently reside in Belleville, Illinois. Besides history and Napoleon, his hobbies include music (he plays the bagpipes, and ragtime piano) and watching his sons play baseball. Tim is 41.

The Three Napoleonic Collections At Brown University
by Peter Harrington
Curator, Anne S. K. Brown Military Collection
Brown University, Providence, R.I.

The Special Collections division of Brown University Library which is housed in the John Hay Library contains three collections dealing with Napoleon and related material. Two are purely Napoleonic in nature while the third - the Anne S. K. Brown Military Collection - contains a vast amount of material on Napoleon and the wars in Europe 1792-1815.

Of the three, the Bullard Napoleon Collection is the smallest in terms of volume of material. In 1942, Paul R. Bullard presented a number of volumes on Napoleon, a bronze bust by R. Colobo, a death mask, and 185 contemporary cartoons, the latter the result of forty years of collecting. The majority of the caricatures are English, one of the earliest being 'Austrian Bugaboo, Funking the French Army' which was published on May 12, 1792. It shows the Austrian Army as a grotesque figure smoking a pipe and blowing smoke at the French soldiers who are falling over each other. There are numerous caricatures by the prolific anti-Napoleonic caricaturist, James Gillray along with works by George Cruikshank and others. This collection is still being added to.

Housed in its own distinctive room, the Hoffman Napoleon Collection was presented to Brown University in 1921 by Mira Hoffman, the widow of the collector, William Henry Hoffman. It consists of books, autographs, prints of battles and scenes, portraits, medals and coins and objects of art. While the majority of books are in the English language, their bindings are particularly attractive.

Perhaps the finest portrait is an oil painting on panel by Horace Vernet. This is said to have been Napoleon's favorite portrait and one which he took on many journeys. Later he gave it to his surgeon, Barry O'Meara, on St. Helena who in turn gave it to the Irish poet, Thomas Moore. The medals commemorate events such as the marriage of Napoleon and Marie Louise, the Battles of Eylau, Moscova, Jena, and other victories, and various coronation medals. Many famous European statesmen and soldiers are represented in the autograph collection ranging from letters by Alexander I, Ney, Wellington, Davout, Queen Hortense, Louis XVIII, and the Emperor himself.

The largest holdings on Napoleon and the wars in Europe, 1792-1815, can be found in the Anne S. K. Brown Military Collection. This was formed over a period of forty years by the late Mrs. John Nicholas Brown (1906-1985) and is still being added to. It contains approximately 30,000 volumes (books, portfolios, scrapbooks, albums, etc) and 60,000 prints, drawings and watercolours, as well as a collection of 5,000 miniature lead soldiers. The entire collection (which was probably the largest private military collection in the world) was presented to Brown University and transferred to the John Hay Library in 1982.

The original emphasis was the history and illustration of world military uniforms, circa 1500-1918, but it now contains in addition, a vast amount of material on military and naval history, military and naval arts and tactics, campaigns, ceremonies and royalty, biography, portraiture and caricatures, covering the period. It contains manuscripts, original photographs, posters and other graphic documentation.

While most major countries are represented, the section on France is one of the largest. In terms of the graphics relating to the Napoleonic era, there are hundreds of prints, drawings and watercolours representing battles, portraits, uniformed figures, caricatures and other scenes. There is a sketchbook kept by Faber du Four during the retreat from Moscow and another sketchbook by Meissonier, along with numerous watercolours by, among others, Vernet, Detaille, Martinet, and Rousselot. There is an interesting group of original photographs of Napoleonic veterans taken in Paris in the 1850's.

Included are many books on Napoleon, his army, and campaigns ranging from large illustrated portfolios to a minute album of original guaches paintings of his battles. The various ceremonies and coronations of the Emperor and other European royalty are represented in a unique collection of large fete books. There are printed regulations for the period along with drill and tactical treatises. The wars of Napoleon are represented in other sections such as Russia, Britain, the Netherlands and Prussia. There are many collections of watercolours and prints of uniforms of the period in these sections as well as campaign and regimental histories, army lists, drill books, and military biography. All in all, the Military Collection probably has the largest coverage of the Napoleonic Wars outside Europe.

Material from all three collections can be examined by permission, and the main reading room of the Military Collection which houses the model soldiers as well as prints and paintings on the walls, can be viewed at any time between Monday and Friday, 9.00 AM to 5.00 PM. Photocopying of material is permitted depending on the condition of the binding and it is also possible to microfilm books. Photographs can be made from items in the collections if they are for private research. There is a reproduction fee for commercial projects. Enquiries should be directed to The Curator, Anne S. K. Brown Military Collection, Box A, Brown University Library, Providence, Rl 02912-0001.

• • •

Peter Harrington, a native of Manchester, England, studied History and Archaeology in London and Edinburgh before coming to Brown University in 1981˜ to pursue a degree in Museum Studies. Since 1983 he has worked in the Anne S.K. Brown Military Collection and in 1990 became curator. He is an authority on the iconography of war and has written extensively on the subject. His other research interest is the archaeology of war.

Napoleonic Nobility And Its Offshoots
by Derwin Mak, Toronto, ONT.

1. Legitimate Nobility vs. Napoleonic Nobility

What is nobility, and how did Napoleon change it? First, we must define "nobility." The nobility is the upper social class of hereditary or life-long titles and ranks.

Nobility emerged after the collapse of the Roman Empire. The first nobles were the tribal chiefs of the Germanic and Asiatic tribes which wandered all over Europe.

These tribes - such as the Goths, the Visigoths, the Franks, the Magyars and the Huns - were warlike peoples, and so their leaders were the most brutal, violent warriors in the tribe.

Many of our modern titles of nobility have their origins as the titles of warrior chiefs. For example, Duces or Dukes were originally Roman commanders, and the barbarians adopted the Latin name for their own use. The English title "Earl" is derived from the Danish word "jarl," which was a military viceroy in England.

As the feudal system emerged, the military obligations to the tribe became hereditary, and so did the titles. But as the feudal system developed, the military rule of the nobility decreased. The nobles conquered large territories and estates for themselves, and so they controlled the land, and therefore, the economies of their states and tribes. They no longer needed to control people and wealth by military force alone - they could now control society by controlling agriculture and trade. They could do less of the fighting and hire lesser nobles, such as the knights, or even peasants to do their fighting. And since the land and titles were hereditary, generation after generation of noblemen inherited the wealth to hire private armies to fulfil their military obligations to their king.

By the time of the Renaissance, the nobility had ceased to have any military role except the ceremonial. Then, centuries later, Napoleon challenged the basic concepts of European nobility.

Napoleon awarded knighthoods and titles to peasant and noble alike - he did not discriminate due to birthright. Napoleonic knighthoods and titles were rewards for military, and later, civil merit. This type of nobility appealed strongly to all soldiers from privates up to generals and to all citizens from the peasants up to the middle class.

But not to the established, pre-Napoleonic nobility. Their monopoly on power based on birthright was threatened by Napoleon's power based on merit. Of course, the two types of nobility fought each other from 1804 to 1815. Ironically, Napoleon had actually brought nobility back to its origins.

Thus, by the beginning of the nineteenth century, two types of nobility fought for control of Europe: the legitimists and the Napoleonic nobility. The legitimists were the old aristocracy, and they claimed their elite status based on hereditary succession to hereditary titles existing before the French Revolution. The Napoleonic nobility claimed their status based on rewards from Napoleon for their achievements.

Ironically, almost all legitimist royal and noble families had non-legitimate origins. Almost every one of them had seized power in a palace coup, an assassination or an uprising. The Grimaldis, for example, became the royal family of Monaco by assassinating the ruler of Monaco. But unlike Napoleon, the legitimate nobility were willing to overlook their own origins and falsify some family trees to support their regimes.

Incidentally, the war between legitimist and Napoleonic nobility did not end at Waterloo. As recently as 1966, feuding broke out between supporters of the Bourbon, Orleans and Bonaparte royal families at the International Congress of Genealogical and Heraldic Sciences in Paris. Supporters of these rival royal families held their own meetings and parties and issued pamphlets attacking each other's views.

Napoleon, despite his constant warfare against the legitimate nobility, tried to ingratiate himself to them, imitated them, and may have wanted to become one of them. He was like a *parvenu* who had just recently climbed into the next social class.

Despite his stated mission to reward people for their achievements, he handed out kingdoms to his siblings, none of whom showed any civil or military merit. He was committing the worst crime of the old nobility, the granting of titles by birthright.

Napoleon schemed to legitimize his dynasty by marrying it to the old nobility, as if it were important to be linked by marriage to established monarchs. In 1807, he arranged for His brother Jerome to marry Friedricke Catharina Sophie Dorothea, daughter of the King of Wurttemburg - a King made by Napoleon, but nevertheless, the head of an ancient line of Dukes.

Napoleon himself divorced his non-royal wife Josephine and married the Archduchess Marie Louise of Habsburg, thus tying the newest imperial family to the oldest in 1810.

And then there was Napoleon's coronation, an event which was gaudier and more theatrical than any coronation of the old nobility. Despite his dislike of the old nobility, he certainly imitated it and tried to join it.

2. Surviving Royal Houses Established by the Bonapartes

The Bonaparte emperors, Napoleon I and his nephew Louis Napoleon or Napoleon III, installed several royal families, some of which still survive:

2.1. The House of Murat

The royal family founded by Joachim Murat, son of an innkeeper, later Marshal of the Empire, and finally, King of Naples, still survives. The current Prince, Joachim Murat, was a campaign aide to President Valerie Giscard d'Estaing.

2.2. The House of Wittelsbach (Bavaria)

Duke Albrecht of Bavaria is the current head of the House of Wittelsbach.

Before 1806, the Wittelsbachs were Electors of Bavaria and the Holy Roman Empire. In 1806, with the end of the Holy Roman Empire and the creation of the Confederation of the Rhine, Napoleon elevated

Bavaria to the status of a sovereign kingdom. Maximillian, formerly Elector of Bavaria, became King of Bavaria — a puppet king, but a king nevertheless.

The puppet, however, switched to the allied side before the Battle of Leipzig. This was a smart move: it enabled him to retain his royal status when barqaining with the legitimate monarchs at the Congress of Vienna.

2.3. The House of Wurttemburg

The House of Wurttemburg still exists, now led by Duke Carl of Wurttemburg.

Before 1805, the Wurttemburgs were mere Dukes. But they sided with Napoleon, and the Treaty of Pressburg elevated Wurttemburg to a sovereign kingdom - in reality, another German puppet state of Napoleon's.

Like the King of Bavaria, though, the King of Wurttemburg switched to the allied side, in Wurttemburg's case, after the Battle of Leipzig, and so he was able to keep his royal status after the Congress of Vienna.

The third German royal family elevated by Napoleon, the House of Wettin, royal family of Saxony, stayed loyal to Napoleon. Miraculously, the King Friedrich Augustus of Saxony kept his royal status and his country after the Congress of Vienna.

Like the Bavarian Wittelsbachs, the Wettins were Electors of the Holy Roman Empire, in Saxony. In 1806, Napoleon rewarded the Elector of Saxony by elevating him to King of Saxony.

King Friedrich Augustus remained loyal to Napoleon at the Battle of Leipzig. Unfortunately, his soldiers did not, and they deserted to the allied side and let their king get captured. How the king retained his royal status and kingdom will be described later.

The German Napoleonic kingdoms are notable because the custom of not crowning the King at the coronation began in these states. The Kings of Bavaria, Wurttemburg and Saxony were the first kings to let their crowns sit beside them on a stool beside the throne at the coronation. They realized all too well that they ruled by the grace of Napoleon and not by the grace of God, and they dared not have their clergymen place the crown on their heads. Today, most

Western European monarchies, such as Denmark, Spain and the Netherlands, have adopted this custom and do not actually crown their monarchs at the enthronement ceremony.

2.5. The Imperial House of Habsburg of Mexico

The Imperial House of Habsburg, the royal house of Joseph II and Marie Louise, still survives, headed by Dr. Otto von Habsburg, a member of the European Parliament. But its Napoleonic associations extend after 1815. In 1862, a Habsburg prince was set up as Emperor of Mexico by Napoleon III, Napoleon I's nephew and founder of the Second Empire.

In 1862, France invaded Mexico. Napoleon III, like his uncle, tried to control his territory by establishing a puppet or sympathetic government in Mexico. He convinced Archduke Maximilian, brother of Emperor Franz Josef, that the Mexicans wanted an Emperor and that this was the golden opportunity to establish an empire for himself. In 1864, Maximillian went to Mexico and became Emperor of Mexico.

The Mexican Empire lasted less than three years. Maximillian never controlled all of Mexico, and he and his French troops constantly lost territory to Benito Juarez from the moment he arrived. In 1867, the Mexicans captured and executed Maximilian, who had been abandoned by Napoleon III. The Mexican adventure did not endear the Bonapartes to the Habsburgs.

2.6. The House of Berndadotte (Sweden)

Last but not least, is the only Napoleonic royal family still ruling a kingdom: the House of Bernadotte, now led by King Carl XVI Gustav and his Queen Sylvia.

The great coat of arms of Sweden, i.e., the coat of arms for personal use of the King, shows the Napoleonic coat of arms granted to Marshal Bernadotte in a small centre shield. The King of Sweden is the only ruling monarch who still uses a Napoleonic coat of arms.

3. The Offshoots of Napoleon

In addition to the Napoleonic royal houses, there were also some emperors who blatantly and shamelessly imitated Napoleon.

3.1. Emperor Jacques I of Haiti

The first of these offshoots was Emperor Jacques I of Haiti. The French colony in Haiti erupted into a slave revolt after the fall of the

French monarchy in 1792. By 1804, one of the leaders of the slave rebellion, Jean Jacques Dessalines, had become ruler of the entire French part of Haiti (The Spanish part of the island stayed under Spanish rule and eventually became the Dominican Republic.

In August 1804, Dessalines heard that Napoleon had declared himself Emperor. Dessalines quickly followed suit. He got his personal bodyguard to declare him Emperor of Haiti on September 22, 1804, and then he doctored and backdated official documents to make his empire appear to precede Napoleon's.

Dessalines then rushed to get himself crowned before Napoleon, and he did. Dessalines was crowned Emperor Jacques I of Haiti on October 8, 1804, seven weeks before Napoleon's coronation.

The Empire of Haiti lasted two years. In 1806, Emperor Jacques was assassinated by his own officers.

3.2. Emperor Bokassa I of the Central African Empire

The most flamboyant imitator of Napoleon was Emperor Bokassa I of the Central African Empire. He was most certainly one of Africa's bloodiest dictators and may have been a cannibal. He was also one of Africa's greatest admirers of Napoleon.

Jean Bidel Bokassa was an African soldier in the French Army. He had a stunning military career: he fought in the Indochina War, became a captain, received the Croix de Guerre and became a member of the Legion of Honour, the order founded by Napoleon.

When the Central African Republic became independent from France, Bokassa became one of its military chiefs. Then in 1966, he seized power in a coup.

However, Bokassa was not happy as President for Life. He had always admired French civilization, especially the Age of Napoleon, and in 1977, he announced that he was turning his small republic into the Central African Empire. He spent one quarter of his country's national budget on a coronation modelled after Napoleon's.

It was the most flamboyant coronation since the coronation of Napoleon himself. Bokassa ordered a giant Napoleonic eagle throne built in France. Napoleonic robes, complete with golden bees and eagles, were worn by Bokassa and his new Imperial court. Bokassa and his wife Catherine rode to their coronation in a replica of the carriage used by Napoleon and Josephine to ride to their own coronation.

The coronation was deliberately staged and photographed to resemble David's painting of Napoleon crowning Josephine. And of course, Bokassa crowned himself Emperor of the Central African Empire.

The Central African Empire lasted less than two years. Bokassa was overthrown by his cousin in 1979.

4. After the Congress of Vienna

One of the goals of the Congress of Vienna, convened in 1814 by the victorious allies, was to sort out who was royal and who wasn't. The losers were the Bonapartes and the Murats since the legitimists considered these two royal families to be commoners and usurpers. Paradoxically, the legitimate monarchs recognized the kings of Bavaria and Wurttemburg as legitimate monarchs as a reward for their defection to the allied side, and so two legitimate royal families were created by illegitimate means.

The allies were not sure what to do with the king of Saxony. He was still loyal to Napoleon. The Czar of Russia wanted to give Saxony to Prussia in exchange for Prussian Poland. Austria, however, did not want a newly enlarged and powerful Prussia so close to her borders. Thanks to Austria, two-thirds of Saxony was given to Prussia, but the remaining one third was kept as an independent kingdom with King Frederick Augustus still on his throne. Thus a third Napoleonic German king kept his royal status.

It would seem that legitimate monarchy and nobility had returned to Europe and that the Napoleonic concept of nobility had died. But ironically, it was the old concept of nobility, not the Napoleonic concept, which died at the Congress of Vienna.

By allowing three Napoleonic German monarchs to retain their royal status, the allies had silently admitted that the Napoleonic method of creating kings and nobles, while contrary to their own methods, was as legitimate as hereditary succession.

Secondly, all the allied nations created honours and knighthoods based on merit instead of birthright after 1815. Not only did France continue to award the Legion of Honour, but other prestigious orders and decorations were created for commoners and nobles alike: the

Victoria Cross, the Order of the British Empire, the Iron Cross, and the Order of Canada, which does not have any titled nobility, yet is awarded by a monarchy. Two recent examples of commoners who received post-Napoleonic knighthoods for civil or military merit are: Ed Mirvish, a Toronto department store owner who became a Commander of the Order of the British Empire for restoring the Old Vic Theatre in London; and General Norman Schwarzkopf, who recently became an Honourary Knight Commander of the Order of the Bath.

Even the titled nobility changed. Virtually all the allied nations slowed their creation of hereditary titles after 1815, and the British introduced a new type of nobility: the life peer. A life peerage is a noble title given to a person as an award for great merit, but the title expires with the person's death and is not hereditary. Thus, Napoleon's greatest enemy has realized that merit is not hereditary. The few British titles which are created today are all life peerages; the British monarchy has created very few hereditary titles of nobility in the twentieth century.

Why did the allied nations adopt the Napoleonic concept of nobility after having spent eleven years fighting it? Perhaps they realized that Napoleonic nobility had a strong appeal to the middle classes and commoners of their own states, and that they too had to recognize achievement instead of birthright. And so Napoleon had won his war against the old nobility in the end.

• • •

Derwin Mak is a Canadian Chartered Accountant who graduated with a Master of Accounting degree from the University of Waterloo in Waterloo, Ontario. He is also a heraldist and expert on international royalty and has met vice-regal and royal personalities including the Lieutenant-Governor of British Columbia and King Michael of Romania. He is a member of the Heraldry Society of Canada, the Heraldry Society (U.K.), the American College of Heraldry, the Augustan Society and the Monarchist League of Canada. He is the second Chinese Canadian to receive a grant of arms from the Canadian Heraldic Authority, the official heraldic agency of the Canadian monarchy.

In "Defense" of Napoleon—
Napoleon's Domestic Legacy
by J. David Markham, Phoenix, AZ

The title of my talk tonight came out of discussions with President Snibbe that we should consider some of Napoleon's accomplishments. I came up with an unfortunate title, because to me, and no doubt to you, Napoleon really needs no defense. And yet, perhaps he does. While there is something about Napoleon that can be an inspiration to many of us, that response is not universal. I remember reading a Scope and Sequence Report for a high school's world history class (not the one where I now teach) and discovering that it talked about the need to understand the "dictatorship" of Napoleon. I pored over the sections regarding other absolute leaders, including Louis XIV, Henry VIII, and a wide assortment of kings, queens and emperors, and no other such leader was referred to as a "dictator." Only Hitler, Stalin, and Mussolini were given that dubious distinction. I objected most strenuously, but to no avail. More recently, one of my students took note of my interest, and wanted to know if Napoleon was my favorite dictator.

I have also done some recent research into the image of Napoleon as seen in high school world history textbooks. While a number of them are positive or at least neutral, some are rather hostile. One, for example, includes a class project of putting Napoleon on trial. To be fair, it presents a good defense, but the very notion that he should go on trial is, to say the least, rather prejudicial

This image is not, of course, limited to today. George Brandes tells us that Napoleon was often seen as a sort of Faustian "superman," and the term is not meant to flatter. Napoleon was the target of unceasing attack by the caricature artists of the time. In these, he lost his humanity and was seen as the devil or his off-spring. He was the "ogre of Corsica," a butcher without parallel. All of the almost 2 million dead from 15 years of war were laid at his feet. He was seen as a liar, a coward, a foreign usurper. For many today, this image persists.

Of course, extremes in the other direction have also existed. During the July Revolution of 1830 and the time of King Louis–Philippe Napoleon was almost deified. Indeed, some of the art from this time, such as the famous scene of Napoleon welcoming his son to Paradise, make one wonder if Napoleon was being proposed for sainthood. If I had to choose between the two extremes, I'd opt for sainthood, but a more reasonable middle ground does exist. A saint he was not, but he may well have been, in the words of Carlyle, "Europe's Last Great Man."

There is another problem in the perception of Napoleon today, and that is our temptation to judge the early 19th century by the standards of the late 20th century, especially our own liberal democracy. A good example of this is the complaint that Napoleon was not a true democrat, and did not guarantee the type of freedoms that we know today. But I remind you that the Constitution of the United States did not abolish slavery, allowing only white landowning males to vote, and then only for the House of Representatives.

Part of Napoleon's problem today, as it was back in the early 19th century, was his proximity to the French Revolution. Napoleon was a direct result of that great event. To many, this would be a positive feature, as it was the French Revolution that ushered in the process of the dissolution of the old and corrupt regimes and gave us some of the noblest ideals of human history. But to others, the French Revolution was bloodshed, turmoil, and chaos. That it certainly was to the ruling powers of Europe, and so it is with irony that the French Revolution both gave Napoleon his start and made it impossible for the other rulers of the day to fully accept him. Indeed, Napoleon was hated first and foremost because he represented the sweeping change brought on by the French Revolution. It was not, I must all too often remind some of my colleagues, Napoleon who started the Continental Wars. They were started while Louis XVI was still king, and grew out of the desire to carry the ideals of the French Revolution throughout Europe.

Tonight, I am going to discuss some specific accomplishments that I feel we should emphasize in our "defense" of Napoleon. And I am going to proceed from a different perspective than is often taken. In the movie *Waterloo*, one of his aides tells him that he "extended the limits of glory." I don't know if he was ever actually told that, but while we often emphasize the military glory of his conquests, they were in many ways the least important of his accomplishments. We may be inspired by the sound of the heavy drums, the images of grand cavalry charges, and the sight of Napoleon astride his white horse *Marengo*, but Napoleon's legacy goes far beyond that.

I was going to discuss both Napoleon's domestic and foreign accomplishments. Indeed, I did a fair amount of research on some major international accomplishments, and their implications for the Europe of today. Then I decided you didn't want to be here all night. Perhaps at some point at some other conference I will be able to give you my thoughts on *Napoleon and the European Community*.

So this evening, we will consider only a few of Napoleon's specific domestic accomplishments. Through all of these run the common threads of imagination, skill, and inspiration. Through all also runs the spirit of the French Revolution—not the terror with its overuse of the national razor, but rather the ideal of *liberté, egalité* and *fraternité*. The idea that the people of Europe could be free of the old regimes and in a system that rewarded the meritorious and condemned the despotic.

Even with the authoritarianism that came with the Empire, I submit that the impact of Napoleon's heritage was to further the dreams of those idealists of the Revolution.

France during the Revolution was always in turmoil, and this was certainly true during the Directory. The government did not have the support of the people and was doomed long before Napoleon agreed to participate in the *coup d'etat de Brumaire* (November 9-10, 1799).

With this action, Napoleon brought a level of stability unseen for over 10 years. It was in the context of this stability that all of the other accomplishments of Napoleon were possible.

Shortly after the *coup d'etat de Brumaire*, the following poster appeared on the streets of Paris:

France desires something great and of lasting value. Instability has brought her to her knees; she now appeals for stability. She does not want a monarchy; this has been outlawed. But she does expect uniformity in the actions of the authorities charged with implementing the laws. She desires a free and independent Legislative Assembly...she wishes to be represented by peaceable conservatives and not by turbulent reformers; she wishes at last to reap the reward of ten years of sacrifice.

Whatever else may be said of Napoleon, he certainly fulfilled the wishes of the writer of that poster.

Herbert Fisher in his book *Bonapartism* tells us:

Napoleon brought to the task of government exactly that assemblage of qualities which the situation required, an unsurpassed capacity for acquiring technical information in every branch of government, a wealth of administrative inventiveness which has never been equalled, a rare power of driving and draining the energies of men, a beautiful clearness of intellect which enabled him to seize the salient features of any subject, however tough, technical and remote, a soldierly impatience of verbiage in others combined with a serviceable gift of melodramatic eloquence in himself; above all, immense capacity for relevant labor.

It may be that Napoleon's greatest strength was that once he established a goal he never wavered from pursuit of that goal. This could, on occasion, lead to excess, but it is one reason for his tremendous success.

When Napoleon took power in 1799, perhaps the most important thing he did was establish the idea of a strong leader. The Directory had been weak largely because no one was really in a position to make major decisions. Some wanted the Consulate to be run the same way, but Napoleon refused. Critics have complained that this was a sure indication that he was power hungry, but here again we ignore our own history. We tried a weak system under the Articles of Confederation, and for our effort we got 11 years of stagnation and futility. It was only after the creation of a strong central government that the United

States was able to embark on a path that would lead to its greatness. Indeed, it is no accident that Napoleon was a great fan of George Washington. When Washington died, Napoleon put the army on ten days mourning and delivered a eulogy. When the national elections confirmed him as Premier Consul, he ordered the statues of some of the great men of history erected in the gallery of the Tuileries; men such as Alexander, Cicero, Cato, Caesar, Prince Eugene, Frederick the Great, Mirabeau, and George Washington.

It is sometimes said that Napoleon ran the government without regard for democratic principles or procedures. Yet the evidence is to the contrary. The Council of State would debate policy and Napoleon would only give his opinion late in the debate. His questions were insightful, focusing on the justice and usefulness of an issue, and its history. The record indicates that he almost always abided with the majority vote, though he was not required to do so. His only real requirement was hard work; they would often meet all night. Once when the Councillors were napping (no pun intended) he admonished them to stay awake, noting that it was only two o'clock in the morning!

The Consulate, and later the Empire, may have been a strong centralized rule, but compared to previous governments it was a reign of freedom. It gave France a government of regular, scientific and civilized administration in place of near anarchy. Sacrifices of liberty were balanced by gains in equality and safety, and in the restoration of economic stability. Moreover, Napoleon established the principle of popular sovereignty through the repeated use of the plebiscite. If the government was centralized. that was merely the tradition of France to the 15th century, and a tradition that continues today. *Liberté* under Napoleon exceeded that under the monarchs of the rest of Europe. If we question Napoleon's commitment to the rights of the people, we have only to recall his letter to Jerome, King of Westphalia, when he said: "Be a constitutional king. It is necessary that your subjects should enjoy a degree of liberty, equality and well-being unknown to the people of Germany." Later, he wrote "If I had won in 1812, my constitutional reign would have begun."

Napoleon provided more *egalité* than anywhere else in Europe.

Taxes based on ability to pay, inheritance laws that favored equality, government scholarships to help needy students of the middle class: all these shone against the despotic rule of others. Napoleon staked his future on the principle that every man could rise as far as his ability could carry him. In the military, this found support in his statement that in every soldier's knapsack is found a Marshal's baton. In civilian life, he defended the rights of peasants and emigrés alike, and granted all men the opportunity to excel in his empire. The Legion of Honor, despite the fears of its detractors, did not create a new caste. Instead, it reinforced the notion that all men could rise as far as their talents would take them. His removal of the benefits of caste and privilege, the granting of freedom of religion, and a new economic order sent terror into the hearts of the monarchs of Europe, a terror that led to the vilification of the man and to a series of efforts to depose him.

As for *fraternité*, he reunified the French, solved many domestic problems, and restored law and order. He made the French proud to be French, and directed their energies toward national improvements. Felix Markham tells us that "for the first time since 1789...France felt the impulse of a powerful, unified will."

For the ten years of the Revolution, the financial situation in France was chaotic. She was over 300 million francs in the red, and sinking fast. There is a well known story that Napoleon once wanted to know the number of men in the army. The official he questioned did not know, so Napoleon said that he could find out from pay rolls. 'We do not pay the Army" was the reply. Well, how about the ration lists? 'We don't feed the army." Lists of clothing? 'We don't clothe it." The army was not, in fact, being paid. You may recall that a similar situation once existed in the US, and Washington himself had to prevent senior veterans of the Army of the Republic from staging a revolt.

Napoleon immediately raised millions of francs from foreign bankers and a national lottery. He then set about reforming the entire tax system. Taxes had been collected by part time workers: Napoleon created a special cadre of collectors, eight for each *département* (similar to America's states). These officials were required to pay as much as 5 per cent of expected revenue in advance, thus improving the cash flow. The *Département* Vosges was the first to pay up the full amount due, and the lovely *Place des Vosges* is thus named in its honor. Napoleon's improvements in the income tax system led to the elimination of virtually all debt and put the country on sound financial footing. He also added taxes on wine, playing cards, carriages, salt, and tobacco. It seems he had no one whining "read my lips" and "no new taxes," and was thus able to get done what needed to be done. Of course, Napoleon's thrift is legendary: he hated debt, interest payments, and extravagance. He often checked for overspending personally, and later formed an audit office to investigate even the smallest of expenditures.

Perhaps Napoleon's greatest, and longest lasting, financial achievement was the establishment of the Bank of France. This bank allowed France to eliminate high interest rates for its own loans, and brought additional stability to the financial situation. Within one year, the debacle that had been France's finances was no more.

Beyond finances, Napoleon's most famous domestic accomplishment was his legal work. France had not been completely unified all that long, and the system of laws that had emerged was an unbelievable tangle. There were countless regional codes, courts, case law, almost 15,000 decrees, often contradictory, and other documents. Napoleon once wrote "we are a nation with 300 books of laws yet without laws." It is true that Napoleon did not write the entire "revision," but he did preside at most of the meetings of lawyers, and he got his way on numerous points, especially in the Civil Code. This Code reflected the needs of the middle-class, who had most benefitted from the Revolution and who needed assurances that their gains would last. He codified their right to keep lands gained as a result of the Revolution, thus insuring that one of their most important gains would be maintained. He increased the power of the family, and thus returned to Roman legal beliefs. He did not, however, get his way on every effort to expand the power of the family, or to increase its obligations. The Code does reflect his wishes when it declares 'The wife owes obedience to her husband," but some of his remarks indicate that he never really expected very many women to pay much attention to this admonishment. He supported the right to divorce. But with strong restrictions, and in fact very few divorces in Paris occurred in his time.

The Code provided for other things as well, of course, including the right of men to enter any trade, craft, profession or religion they chose. The Code was a judicial compromise between democratic ideals and the monarchy. The Civil Code also returned the right of litigants to seek professional counsel - a right that had been removed in Revolutionary France. The black market being what it always is, this prohibition had simply led to larger fees for advice surreptitiously given.

Because of Napoleon's personal and powerful interest, for the first time in French history there was a unity of law. This unity of law is absolutely critical if a country is to rise to the greatness that is only possible when the nation is completely unified. It is, therefore, completely appropriate that this system of laws became known as the "*Code Napoléon,*" and it is in many ways his most lasting legacy. It remains the basis of French law, as well as the law of Belgium and Luxembourg, and has greatly influenced the law of Western Europe, Mexico, Latin America, Japan, and Louisiana. There have, of course, been changes. In France, for example, there is no longer a fine of 300 francs for having a mistress!

Napoleon did far more than simply cause the Code to be written. He created an entirely new legal system; a system based on merit rather than family connection. His system of prefects brought order and stability to the *départements.* Most of his appointments were men of revolutionary heritage, and none had strong family connections to the *départements.* Napoleon seldom interfered with their activity; one example I found was when he overrode a prefect's effort to censor a local opera.

Napoleon followed the same merit system in his appointment of judges. Civil liberties were protected by the use of petty juries and through the publicity of trials. Indeed, his approach to the entire legal system was among the most liberal of the day, and met with the approval of the revolutionaries and such future critics as Madame de Staël.

One of the most overlooked domestic accomplishments of

Napoleon was his work in educational reform. Education was high on Napoleon's list of priorities, priorities which were in large part those of the middle class. For his merit system to be effective, education must be available to most people, or, in early 19th century Europe, at least to most men. Moreover, the state of French education was not all that it could have been when Napoleon began to rule. A survey conducted in March of 1801 exposed numerous complaints regarding the lack of schools in many areas, lack of professionalism among teachers, lack of discipline and attendance by the students and, in a few areas, the lack of religious education.

Secondary education was extremely important to Napoleon, as it was the base education for the future leaders of the nation. The state had a strong interest in the curriculum being presented, and control would be easier if France established a system of secondary schools under the direction of a central authority. Covering students roughly from ages 10-16, these schools would provide education designed to prepare students for higher level schooling. Indeed, some bonus plans were established for teachers who had large numbers of students qualifying for advancement.

The heart of the new system was the establishment of thirty *Lycées,* or high schools. Every appellate court district was to have a *Lycée,* and they were to be completely supported, and controlled, by the state. Scholarships were provided, with about one third going to sons of the military and government, and the rest for the best pupils from the secondary schools. Each *Lycée* had a six year term of study. The curriculum included languages, modern literature, science, and all other studies necessary for a "liberal" education.

It is clear that the new system of education introduced by Napoleon had more than one purpose. It was intended, of course, to provide an educated elite that could help run the country and the military. It was also designed to provide for an increased middle class: a middle class that would be successful and hence non-revolutionary. Moreover, there was a great emphasis on patriotism in the schools: an emphasis that was to increase during the years of the empire. This is not surprising, of course, as even in modern America we are expected to teach a certain amount of patriotism in our classes: witness the

Pledge of Allegiance and courses in "free enterprise." By our standards, there may have been too much politicization of the educational system. But the standardization of the curriculum, provisions for well-stocked libraries, and a desire to provide all of the capable boys with educational opportunity were all admirable goals. Napoleon's accomplishments in French education, like his work on the Civil Code, are among the greatest of his lasting legacies.

If institutions survive as a lasting legacy, building projects may be even more obvious. Time will not permit a complete compilation of his public works, but a discussion of his legacy would be incomplete without at least a skeletal consideration. Napoleon wanted to increase the unity of France, and key to that unity was communication and transportation. Thus, Napoleon built canals that connected Nantes and Brest, the Rhone and the Rhine. He built three great ports: Cherbourg, Brest, and Antwerp. His three roads through the Alps opened transportation between France, Switzerland, and Italy. Incidentally, some of these roads aren't much better now than they were then. Beyond that, Napoleon spent 277 million on a system of roads throughout France, and he ordered countless trees to protect travelers from the sun. Of course, his triumphal arches and his extension of the Louvre are among the best known of his building projects that have lasted until today.

We can see from our discussion here tonight that Napoleon was a truly remarkable man. His abilities, often seen as being mainly military, go far beyond that important talent. Indeed, he once said "It is not as a general that I am governing France: it is because the nation believes that I possess the civil qualities of a ruler." His abilities as an administrator may well have exceeded his military skills; there can be little doubt that those administrative skills had a longer lasting effect on both France and the world. Napoleon led France, and through her, Europe into the 19th century. This was in spite of the relative shortness of his reign. Imagine the wonderful things he might have done had he had his wish of his days on St. Helena, "If only I had reigned for forty years." His domestic accomplishments provide us with an inspiration that is, or should be, at least the equal of his famous victories on the field of battle. It is these accomplishments that have helped inspire us, as they inspired others.

Goethe: "Now Napoleon-there was a fellow! Always enlightened by reason, always clear and decisive, and gifted at every moment with enough energy to translate into action whatever he recognized as being advantageous or necessary. His life was the stride of a demigod from battle to battle and from victory to victory...it could be said that he was in a permanent state of enlightenment, which is why his fate was more brilliant than the world has ever seen or is likely to see after him."

Talleyrand: "His genius was unbelievable. It is the most astonishing career that has been witnessed for the last thousand years."

Karl Marx: "Camille Desmoulins, Danton, Robespierre, Saint-Just, Napoleon—these were the heroes who, with Roman trappings and phrases, accomplished the mission of their own epoch: they unleashed and established modern bourgeois society. The first four of these smashed feudalism. The fifth, Napoleon, created inside France the conditions that made it possible for free competition to develop, for the redistributed land to be exploited, and for the newly liberated productive energy of the nation to be put to use."

Let me conclude with a passage from Victor Hugo's *Les Misérables*. He is writing about Marius, whose father had fought with Napoleon. This passage perhaps illustrates the effect that Napoleon has had on people up to the present day.

His heart was contracted, he was transported, trembling and gasping; and all alone, without knowing what was within him or what he obeyed, he rose, stretched his arms out of the window, looked fixedly at the shadow, the silence, the dark infinitude, the eternal immensity, and shouted: 'Long live the Emperor!" From this moment it was all over. The ogre of Corsica, the usurper, the tyrant, the monster who was the lover of his own sisters, the actor who took lessons of Talma, the prisoner of Jaffa, the tiger, Bonaparte-all this faded away and made room in his mind for a radiance in which the pale marble phantom of Caesar stood out serenely at an inaccessible height.... He was the predestined constructor of the French group which succeeded the Roman group in the dominion of the universe, he was the prodigious architect of an earthquake, the successor of Charlemagne, Louis XI, Henri IV, Richelieu,

Louis XIV, and the Committee of Public Safety; he had doubtless his spots, his faults, and even his crimes, that is to say, he was a man, but he was august in his faults, brilliant in his spots, and powerful in his crime. ...Marius saw in Bonaparte the dazzling specter which will ever stand on the frontier and guard the future."

Ladies and Gentlemen, it has been an enormous pleasure to speak to you tonight. I thank you for this opportunity and honor, and close with those words that tie us all together:

Vive l'Empereur!

* * *

David Markham is an educator, collector, and student of Napoloen. He has taught high school World History as well as several community colleges and the University of Wisconsin. He holds a Bachelor of Science degree from the University of Iowa, a Master of Arts degree from the University of Northern Iowa, and a Master of Education degree from Arizona State University. He is a member of Alpha Kappa Delta international sociological honor society, and Phi Kappa Phi national honor society.

David is currently serving a three year term on the board of Directors of the Napoleonic Society of America. *He has served as President and Vice-President of the* Allieance Française of Greater Pheonix, *and Vice-President of the* Arizona Committee for the French Revolution. *David was also a board member of the* World Affairs Council of Arizona.

David's collection of snuff boxes, medallions, porcelains, prints and other items relating to Napoleon has achieved wide acclaim. The Pheonix Art Museum featured his collection in their special exhibituon: Napoleon the Great: Selections from the David Markham Collection. *David is currently writing a book on collecting Napoleonic artifacts.*

BORODINO: 1812 AND
180 YEARS LATER, 1992
by Major Wilbur E. Gray, US Army War College, Carlisle, PA

"May it be said of each one of us: 'He fought in that great battle under the gates of Moscow!'"-Napoleon

The Preliminaries

The Battle of Borodino occured on 7 September 1812, some 70 miles west of Moscow, and was to be the decisive battle of the Russian campaign. Napoleonic strategy would demand nothing less. Indeed the very heart of Napoleonic strategy dictated swift, continuous operations that would force the enemy into a single titanic battle where his armies would not only be beaten, but obliterated. Upon completion of this "Strategy of Annihilation", all political, economic and social considerations would simply fall into place as victor dictated terms to loser.

But since the Grande Armeé crossed the Vistula River into Russia on 31 May 1812, decisive battle had eluded Napoleon. Russian Minister of War General Baron Mikhail Barclay de Tolly skillfully evaded French attempts at pitched battle and simply withdrew ever farther into the vastness of the Russian steppes. However militarily sound they might be, Barclay's operations were not politically popular with the Russian nobility. The thought of Moscow falling to the French without a fight was an anathema to them. They pressured Czar Alexander I to appoint sixty seven year old Prince Mikhall Kutusov as the new commander of the Russian armies, which he did on 20 August. Kutusov, fat, immobile, and described by Alexander as "immoral and thoroughly dangerous," immediately declared his intent to stand and give battle. In reality, Kutusov had given Napoleon the chance he had been seeking. Thus it happened that Kutusov's Chief of Staff, General Baron Levin Bennigsen, chose the area around the tiny town of Borodino as the place of battle.

Historian Philip Haythornthwaite described the battle area by noting the Russian deployment:

"Kutusov established his line on a ridge overlooking the Semyenowska Creek, the line punctuated by Borodino and the Semenowskaya and Utitsa villages, with a forward position at Shevardino. Russian engineers had feverishly erected earthwork fortifications with artillery embrasures around Borodino, near Utitsa, on the right flank to cover the fords of the Kolocha River which crossed the field in a northwesterly direction, and three formidable strongpoints: the Shevardino Redoubt, the Great Redoubt and the "Bagration fleches "(arrow shaped earthworks), the latter two on either side of Semenowskaya. Much of the position, particularly the left, was covered by heavy brush and woodland. Deployed behind the earthworks, Kutusov's army had a strong right but overextended left, only Utitsa Woods; both flanks were protected by Cossacks and the entire front was screened by light infantry."

The Russians deployed to fight a defensive battle with Barclay's 1st West Army in the North and General Prince Peter Bagration's 2d West Army in the South. Bagration assigned the two divisions of Lieutenant General Nicolai Tuchkow's III Corps to protect Utitsa, backed up by several thousand *opolchenie*, or militia. Lieutenant General Borosdin's two division VIII Corps secured the fleches while Lieutenant General Nicolai Raewski's VII Corps, also two divisions, defended the Great Redoubt and Semenowskaya. Major General Sievers' single division IV Cavalry Corps supported Raewski. Finally, Bagration controlled a small Reserve consisting of the 2d Cuirassier Division, the 7th (or 2d) Converged Grenadier Division and General Akim Karpow's Cossacks.

Barclay assigned the two divisions of General Dimitri Docturow's VI Corps to defend Gorki. The four divisions of Lieutenant General Karl Baggowout's II Corps and Lieutenant General Aleksandr

Osterman,Tolstoy's IV Corps defended the fords across the northeast trace of the Kolocha River. This latter deployment was a crucial mistake on Barclay's part. The steep banks of the Kolocha virtually assured that the French would not strike that wing of the Russian Army. Barclay supported this defense with three complete cavalry corps - the Ist under Lieutenant General F.P.Uwarow, the IId under Major General F.K.Korff and the IIId under Major General Kreutz. General Matwei Platow added some 5,500 Cossacks. Barclay's Reserve consisted of Grand Duke Constantine's redoubtable V Imperial Guard Corps and Major General Aleksandr Kutaisow's 312 gun Artillery Park.

Kutusov himself seemed to have no other battle plan than to let Barclay and Bagration run the battle as they saw fit. Never-the-less, with between 103,800 and 120,000 men at his disposal, the defense looked strong. However, untrained militia from Smolensk and Moscow numbered some 15,000 of this total. One officer sadly described them as "raw peasants clutching pikes and muskets which they scarcely knew how to wield."

For his part, Napoleon rejected a scheme by Marshal Nicholas Davout for a huge outflanking movement to the south of the Utitsa Forest. Napoleon had concerns that the *Grande Armeé* was simply too weak in numbers to attempt such a movement. The army was already down to somewhere between 124,000 and 134,000 men from the 286,000 that the main force started with at the Vistula. He also feared that the Russians might take to their heels yet again when they discovered the French maneuver. This would deny the Emperor the decisive victory that he so critically needed to win his campaign. Napoleon therefore refused the preferable scheme of a Battle of Maneuver out of hand.

Instead, Napoleon chose to fight a Battle of Attrition. That is, he intended to pound the Russian battleline until it was almost at the breaking point, thus forcing Kutusov to commit all his reserves. At this point Napoleon intended to find and strike, with his own reserves, the weakest part of the Russian line. This action should split the Russian defense in two and collapse Kutusov's army.

French forces captured the Shevardino Redoubt on 6 September, and this allowed Napoleon to examine Russian intentions more closely. This reconnaissance validated the Emperor's battle plan. Napoleon also picked the area around the partially razed village of Semenowskaya as the point where he would rupture the Russian defense. Opposite this point the Emperor planned to deploy nearly 85,000 of the 123,600 men present in his army, all on a front less than a mile and a half wide.

Major General Josef Poniatowski's V Polish Corps got the job of capturing Utitsa and crushing the Russian left flank. Napoleon directed Prince Eugene de Beauharnais' IV Corps to occupy the attention of the Russian right by capturing Borodino. His corps consisted of two infantry divisions, the Royal Italian Guard, 3000 cavalry, and reinforced with two infantry divisions from Davout's I Corps. Eugene was then to transfer the bulk of his corps by pontoon bridge to the southern bank of the Kolocha River and storm the Great Redoubt. Major General Emmanuel Grouchy's III Cavalry Corps deployed to support Eugene. Davout, with 1200 cavalry and two infantry divisions, received orders to capture the *fleches*. Marshal Michel Ney's III Corps, some 1800 cavalry and three infantry divisions, would support Davout's effort. Napoleon held in reserve Major General Friant's division of I Corps, the Imperial Guard, Major General Jean Junot's VIII Westphalian Corps and, finally, Marshal Joachim Murat's Cavalry Reserve. The latter counted nearly 13,000 sabers, consisting of Major General Etienne Nansouty's Ist, Major General Louis-Pierre Montbrun's IId and Major General Nicholas Latour-Maubourg's IV Cavalry Corps. Napoleon would commit these forces as needed.

The Battle

The French were to attack at dawn. Historians recall that as the first rays of light crept across the eastern sky an optimistic Napoleon could remind himself of the "Sun of Austerlitz." Even now, however, problems were beginning to crop up. French artillery had somehow found itself set up outside the range of its targets and had to redeploy. This took a little doing, but at six AM 210 French guns began to belch fire at the *fleches*. The massed artillery heralded what one historian would call "the bloodiest day in military history prior to the First World War."[4]

Prince Eugene's IV Corps quickly swung into action. Major General Morand's Division (attached from I Corps) had deployed south of the Kolocha and swiftly cleared all the Russian light infantry screening the Great Redoubt. North of the Kolocha Major General Delzon's Division immediately overran Borodino, sending the defending Russian Guard *Jagers* scurrying toward Gorki. Delzon mounted a pursuit but the Russian VI Corps defending Gorki forced his retreat back to Borodino. The Russians found the French too powerful to attempt a recapture of Borodino, burning its bridge across the Kolocha instead. Eugene then positioned his artillery around Borodino to bombard the Great Redoubt to his southeast. He also began to transfer the bulk of his infantry and cavalry to the southern bank of the Kolocha to assault the very same fortification.

In the southern part of the battlefield, the difficult underbrush around Utitsa delayed the attack of Poniatowski's Poles until about seven AM. There would be many hours of tough tree-to-tree fighting before the Russians would finally surrender the town in its identically named forest at four PM. Even this would only occur after Napoleon had committed Junot's Westphalians to the fray at nine in the morning. The VII Corps was initially to link Poniatowski with Davout's I Corps in the north, and then clear Utitsa Forest of the enemy light infantry that had been harassing Davout's advance. The Polish attack had certainly begun spectacularly, with the Poles storming and immediately taking the town of Utitsa, fortifications and all. The reason for this success was simple. Bagration had ordered the 3d Division of the Russian III Corps north to reinforce the *fleches*. This detachment left General Tuchkow with only the 1st Grenadier Division to stop the Poles. However, at seven AM Bagration had wisely requested Baggovout's II Corps from the North to reinforce Tuchkow. Upon Baggowout's arrival at ten AM, the battle turned into the seesaw affair that lasted until late in the afternoon.

Obviously, Bagration's reinforcing of the *fleches* told of a serious problem for that position and the Russian center as a whole. The problem was Marshal Davout's two divisions who roared in and captured the southern *fleche* at six AM. Davout personally led the attack after his lead division commander, Major General Compans, went down under a hail of grapeshot. The French attack, spearheaded by "the Terrible" 57th Line Regiment, must have been quite impressive. Bagration himself stood up in his saddle, clapped his hands and shouted "Bravo, bravo!" at the French assault. The attack also impressed Napoleon, who later awarded the coveted Legion of Honor to the entire regiment, the only French unit of the era so honored. Bagration then began to take more practical measures to correct the situation. He requested reinforcements from Kutusov, and when Kutusov would not respond, pleaded directly to Barclay for help. Despite that Barclay and Bagration personally despised each other, the former responded by sending part of the Imperial Guard to the *fleches*. He also ordered Baggowout's II Corps south to reinforce Utitsa. Barclay then threw his reserve grenadiers and heavy cavalry, as well as Tuchkow's 3d Division, against Davout. The counterattack forced Davout to retreat and the Marshal himself became a temporary casualty when his horse was hit by Russian artillery fire.

Meanwhile Marshal Ney, never far from a fight, led his III Corps against the northern *fleche* at about seven AM. The redheaded commander took the position at the first assault, but like Davout, retreated under the counterattack of Bagration's reserves. Attack then followed counterattack, but around ten AM the fortunes of war began to smile on France. Bagration received a round in the leg and after losing much blood toppled from his horse, in plain view of hundreds of Russian infantry. This event completely demoralized the Russian southern wing and gave a final French attack at eleven undisputed control of the *fleches*. Barclay then shifted Tolstoy's IV Corps southward, just to the northwest of Semenowskaya, in an attempt to plug the gap. The Russian situation was becoming critical as the battle was barely four hours old and Kutusov had already seen significant chunks of his reserves committed.

French pressure would not abate, however. Immediately upon seizing the *fleches*, French artillery moved up and began to pound Semenowskaya where the remnants of the Borosdin's VII Corps took refuge. Napoleon then ordered General Friant's division to move out of reserve status and storm the tiny Russian village. Prince Murat supported this attack by deploying Nansouty's I Cavalry Corps to the left of Friant's and Latour-Maubourg's IV Cavalry Corps to his right. As the infantry advanced the cavalry would execute a massive pincer flanking attack designed to trample the Russian forces deployed on either side of the village. The attack succeeded and by twelve o'clock Semenowskaya also fell to the French. Napoleon deployed yet another massed artillery battery around Semenowskaya and these guns began to rake the Great Redoubt from the southern flank. The Russian center was clearly about to split and at twelve o'clock the French Marshals on the scene petitioned the Emperor to commit his reserves, specifically the Young Guard. But as he had done earlier, Napoleon refused saying, "Before I deploy my reserve I must be able to more clearly see my chessboard." Murat took the news gracefully, but Ney was livid. The refusal gave the Russians enough time to reform their forces into a second (shaky) defensive line.

During this time Russian General Raewski's Great Redoubt was the scene of much desperate fighting. Prince Eugene had transferred the bulk of his forces south of the Kolocha. He launched an attack against the redoubt at ten AM using General Broussier's 14th Infantry Division. The attack failed but an attack by General Morand's 1st Division at eleven carried the position. Unfortunately, General Yermalow, Barclay's Chief of Staff, was near the position en route to Semenowskaya with two horse batteries. Yermalow immediately dropped the guns and canistered the rear of the redoubt. Then he and Artillery Reserve Commander Kutaisow grabbed every available infantryman and counterattacked. Their assault was successful but French artillery shot Kutaisow dead. As a result, the entire Artillery Reserve would not move so much as a centimeter for the rest of the battle. Eugene, on the other hand, collected his forces for yet another try at the position.

This next assault would be delayed for three hours, however, as reports began to come in concerning a Russian flank attack in the North. The Russians had evidently found a usable ford across the northwest branch of the Kolocha. Kutusov approved a diversionary attack across the river into the French northern flank, hoping to relieve some of the pressure on the center. Some 8000 cavalry from General Uwarow's I Cavalry Corps and Platow's Cossacks launched the scheme, and this forced Eugene to delay his plans. Eugene shifted sufficient forces north across the Kolocha to deal with the Russians. The Czar's horsemen found themselves easily repulsed with French baggage train guards, among others, sending the Cossacks packing. For the Russians, however, the maneuver was good enough.

Eugene launched the final assault against the redoubt at three o'clock in the afternoon. Three infantry divisions stormed the redoubt from the front while Grouchy's III Cavalry Corps swung to the north of the position to destroy any Russians in the rear. Latour-Maubourg's IV Cavalry Corps and General Caulaincourt's II Cavalry Corps thundered to the South of the position to attack its flank and rear. Caulaincourt had taken control of Montbrun's cavalry when the latter fell to a Russian cannon ball (he clapped and yelled "Good shot!" when he saw the projectile coming toward him). The attack was successful with the infantry pouring over the front of the redoubt and Latour-Maubourg's Saxon cuirassiers spinning left and coming through the rear. The Russians died to the last man.

An initial French advance from the redoubt stalled in the face of Russian artillery. Never-the-less, it was evident that the new, hastily forming Russian line was on the verge of total collapse. Kutusov had not a single reserve formation left to commit. The French marshals present again implored Napoleon to unleash the Imperial Guard to finish the Russians. Though he had some 20,000 untouched troops available, Napoleon thought and then at five PM declined. He stated, "When you are 800 leagues from France, you do not wreck your last reserve." Kutusov withdrew during the night and the drama of Borodino was over.

Aftermath

While Count Leo Tolstoy exaggerated in his description of the battle, it was indeed a bloodbath. French losses were 23,255 men, about 19% of the army present. Russian losses were infinitely worse with some 45,600 casualties, or about 45% of the army on the field. Indeed, Raewsky's corps was down to 700 effectives while one Russian officer mistook the 2d Division as part of a single battalion. The 7th Converged Grenadier Division suffered the most grevious loss with nearly 96% casualties. It is little wonder that Barclay needed constant rum to keep going.

Yet, this battlefield victory was not the decisive victory that Napoleon needed. The Russian army, though beaten senseless, was still intact. As long as the Russian army remained alive, Czar Alexander turned a deaf ear to Napoleon's attempts at negotiations. With winter coming on, and so far from France, the very existence of the Russian Army doomed Napoleon's Russian invasion to failure. Paradoxically, Borodino was the decisive battle primarily because it was not decisive. This would force Napoleon into the disastrous retreat where Cossacks, "Marshal Mud" and "Marshal Winter" would take their toll. Of the 630,000 that began the campaign, only 65,000 would survive the retreat from Moscow. Of these some 35,000 could best be described as little more than stragglers. In this regard, one might well note the Emperor's compliment to the Wurtemburgers on 10 November 1812, where he noticed them still marching in formation. From an initial strength of 4000, the Wurtemburgers now numbered thirty.

But Borodino was important in another way as well. Borodino might well be called the first true expression of Russian nationalism. The Russian soldier fought and died at Borodino not simply because his officers told him to, but because this time it was his fight as well. This war was not simply "the final argument of kings," but a war in which the survival of his culture and his way of life seemed at stake. Borodino signaled to all that affairs of state ceased to be the sole province of the Czar, it concerned the people as well. The people would no longer remain ignored.

At first the Russian government deliberately tried to instill such patriotic concern and fervor into their soldiers to gain the same electric enthusiasm that French soldiers seemed to possess. Ceremonies such as the procession of the icon of the Black Virgin of Smolensk inspired the troops to truly Herculean efforts. The Russian soldier had always been known as a tough customer. One French officer remarked that it was not enough to shoot a Russian soldier, you had to push him over. And at Borodino the legend grew even larger. British General Sir Robert Wilson certainly noticed this when he observed the militia and wrote:

"The very militia who had just joined (and who, being armed only with pikes, formed the third rank to the battalions), not only stood as steady under the cannonade as well as their veteran comrades, but charged the sallying enemy with an ardent ferocity!"

But the advisors to the Czar also recognized the danger of such rampant patriotism. Such enthusiasm might well become insurrection if left unchecked. Thus one Russian partisan leader, Captain Naryshkin, received orders to disarm his own men and "execute those guilty of rebellion!" When Private Chetvertakow raised a partisan force of some 4000 men, the government immediately branded him a troublemaker, arrested him and forced him to return to his regiment. Alas, it was too late for both Czar and noble. Once unleashed, the Russian peoples' love and pride for their country could not be restrained. It would reassert itself in front of the Winter Palace in 1917, and yet again in front of the Russian Federation's Parliament in 1991. Borodino foretold not only the end of Napoleon, but the end of the Russian and Soviet empires as well. That might be considered the battle's greatest legacy.

The Battlefield Today

Today the battlefield at Borodino remains as one of Russia's sacred memorials. The battlefield contains a modern museum with many fine exhibits. Some of the many displays include full scale dioramas, a complete battle map in miniature and dozens of original uniforms. There is even a section dedicated to Tolstoy's rendition of the battle in "*War and Peace.*" The museum also reserves a section for exhibits from the World War II battle near Borodino in 1941.

The battlefield itself remains much the way it was in 1812, and is quite pretty during the spring and summer months. Ceremonies still take place each September 7th, when Czarist colors parade for present day Russian soldier and officer cadets. Every summer, Russian military reenactors hold a military encampment near the battle area as well. Here Russian teenagers are able personally to experience many aspects of the 1812 campaign from the hands of knowledgeable history enthusiasts. The town of Borodino, complete with its attractive onion domed chapel, still exists. Fortifications with period artillery, such as the Bagration *fleches*, remain intact and dot the battle area. Unlike most European battlefields, monuments fill the landscapes of Borodino. Some of the memorials, most built in 1912, include:

> A monument to General Newerowski of the 27th Division.
> A memorial to Prince Kutusov.
> A memorial to the Wolhynia Infantry Regiment.
> A memorial to the Russian Guard *Jagers* and Marines.
> A monument to the 12th Division.
> A monument to the 2d Grenadier Division.
> A monument to the 27th Division.
> A monument to the 2d Cuirassier Division.

A memorial to the Litowski Guard Regiment, which at one point actually bayonet charged French heavy cavalry (losing 741 men out of 1500 in the process).

And finally, a large monument to the Grande Armée of France.

Moscow itself contains perhaps two of the most fascinating Borodino exhibits. Near Poklonnaya Hill stands the majestic Triumphal Arch to the War of 1812, some twenty eight meters high. Nearby stands the Museum of the Borodino Cyclorama with its equally impressive monument to Kutusov out front. Inside stands the magnificent panorama by Russian artist Franz Rubo. Some 115 meters long and 15 meters high, the work accurately depicts the final French assault on Semenowskaya at eleven AM. Visitors swear it is the same as standing in the middle of the burning village itself back in 1812. From the depiction of the infantry and cavalry formations, to the uniforms of the Saxon cuirassiers (who discarded their heavy iron cuirasses before the Russian invasion), the work is world famous for the painstaking research that created it.

Next year (1992) will mark the 180th Anniversary of the Battle of Borodino. Unfortunately, present economic conditions in the former Soviet Union may preclude many of the celebrations planned for this momentous occasion. Regardless, the birth of reform and democracy makes today the best time for a visit to the land of Prince Kutusov. For those of us who are fortunate enough to go, our sojourn will certainly not be complete without a stop at the shrines of Borodino.

* * *

Major Wilbur E. Gray is a Virginia National Guardsman serving with the Strategic Studies Institute, U.S. Army War College, in the capacity of a Strategic Research Analyst and Military Historian. A graduate of the U.S. Army Command and General Staff College, Major Gray holds BA's in both history and political science from Clemson University and an MA in international relations from thje University of Southern California. A military intelligence officer in the Active Guard/Reserve program, he has served in numerous active duty assignments, including a tour with the 1st Armored Division in Germany. His National Guard assignments include positions with the 29th Infantry Division (Light).

In his last assignment as an Assistant Professor of Military Science at the University of Virginia, he taught a course on "Napoleon at War." He is currently working on an article on the 1805 Ulm campaign and a book on Napoleonic strategy.

Napoleon's Cultivation of The Arts–Sculpture

by James Jahnke, Seattle, WA

Every facet of living which could add lustre to Napoleon's conception of *La Gloire* was incorporated into the tapestry of Empire. If proven useful, every colour on the palette of beauty was utilized. Sculpture, like music, architecture, rich and colourful fabrics, furniture, *objets d'art*, everything had its place in Napoleon's conception of what was grand and noble, majestic and yes, hopefully, timeless.

Previously, monarchs thought and acted in terms that were meant to captivate, titillate, and at any given moment, mesmerize. Napoleon, however, intended to penetrate the individual, the nations, the *World*, with the measureless glory of his Empire, not for a time, but for *All Time*.

It follows, that no King could create and maintain all that he envisioned. No, it would take an Emperor to carry out his grandiose schemes, and so became not a King, but an Emperor. Thus, Napoleon cast his glance and his mind on things past for models to achieve his goals, with Rome and Greece the examples he chose to emulate and improve upon.

Along with a brief text for our roundtable discussion, I have included 38 quick-copy examples of sculpture that Napoleon approved of, or would have approved of, had they been executed during his immediate reign. Most are busts or statues, with a few examples of the massive work accomplished on major structures raised during the First Empire or shortly thereafter, since the effects of Napoleon's conceptions were not restricted solely to the period during which he held sway. Nobility, haughtiness, proud demeanor, beauty of line, delicacy of details; all these and more were part and parcel of his effect on sculpture.

There were no cameras, no televisions, and relatively few pictorials to scatter abroad visual images of Napoleon's intended greatness. However, through a massive infusion of portable likenesses of various personages throughout the Empire, along with paintings and drawings, a great world-wide audience was given some idea of who and what was having a significant effect on their lives, and the generations to follow. After all there were uncounted numbers of people who never had the opportunity to cast their gaze directly upon the Emperor, but on his bust, his statue, etc., possibly so. Sculpture for Napoleon was but one element of propaganda, along with its aesthetic and decorative qualities. It was meant to express to the people what the model was like, or as the model intended people to envision him/her. On occasion, the artist depicted the model as he assumed they wished to be viewed. One might almost "hear" stentorian pronouncements issue from the mouth of a Napoleonic bust crowned by the laurel circlet of a Caesar. With, the right tools, especially those of an accomplished artist, mankind was meant to be impressed.

Omniscence, omnipresence, permanence, all of these qualities were meant to be conveyed by the artistry of a score of first-rate artists, with a multitude of secondary examples to accompany the first-rate renditions. Napoleon said that men were attracted by baubles, but these were such baubles as to continue to dazzle mankind so long as we are enthralled by *La Goire, La Gloire de Napoleon*.

When Napoleon Bonaparte rose to political power, he too shared the popular enthusiasm for all that was ancient. His chosen models were Alexander the Great and Julius Caesar, especially the latter since Caesar's career and Napoleon's had so many parallels. Napoleon became first a republican consul; later he ruled France through a tribune; and then, after a plebiscite, he became the modern incarnation of a Roman emperor. The fasces became his symbol of authority; the eagles of the old Roman legions he made into the insignia of the French battalions, and eventually he was crowned with the laurel leaf, or wreath, that ancient symbol of immortal fame. Witness the physical and spiritual transformation in Empire sculpture. Such a manipulation of the forms and images of ancient glory had a vast appeal to this man of modest birth. Coming to power so soon after the demise of an unpopular monarchy, Napoleon had to emphasize that many of the Roman emperors were of equally plebian backgrounds, and that the imperial toga had not necessarily been hereditary.

The sculptors of the Empire period produced works in abundance but in creative vigor they were far inferior to the great painters of the age. This was not because sculptors lacked state patronage, for they also worked in privileged conditions; but there was no great outstanding personage among them of the stature of Gros, David or Ingres. Not even the use of color could give life to their imitative and all too often pedestrian imitations of antique sculpture, which no longer had the charm of the Louis XVI statuary in which elegant neo-Classical stylization was combined with impassioned study of the human figure. The works of Joseph Chinard (1756-1813), perhaps the most talented of Empire sculptors, did not rise above the level of delicate objets d'art, elegant and spirited trifles, or highly-refined knick-knacks, although his terra-cottas were skillfully varnished and his few marble figures finely chiselled and charmingly decorative. The enchanting persuasiveness of his *Madame Recamier*, whom he portrayed in several versions the best being that in the museum in Lyons, is not to everyone's taste. He also flirted with the theme of the Revolution (as in the medallion now in the *Musée Carnavalet*, Paris making her appear more chic by giving her a profile like that of some haughty *ci-devant*, with her carefully studied hair style crowned by a cap with a patriotic cockade somewhat similar to the magnificent ostrich plumes so dear to Marie Antoinette.

For all his charm the elegant Chinard was in no way comparable to Antonio Canova (1757-1822), the finest sculptor of the age, perhaps the last really universal Italian artist, and almost the counterpart in sculpture of David because of his influence on European art of the early 19th century. Magnificent testimonies to his close links with Napoleon and the Imperial family include the portraits of the Emperor that he executed at various times. Napoleon preferred to be figured in uniform, however, Canova persuaded him to pose instead in a pseudo-antique garb. The statue, twelve feet in height, was hewn at St. Cloud in 1808; on completion it was brought to Paris and placed in the Louvre. However, it stayed there only a short while, for Wellington carried it off to England in 1815, where it remains to this day, in Apsley House, London, and the bronze replica in the courtyard of the Brera art gallery in Milan. Another more human and perhaps more convincing portrait of the younger Bonaparte was studied from life during the artist's stay in Paris in 1802 (the original gesso model is at Possagano). His other sitters included Madame Mere, Murat, Caroline, Pauline, Cardinal Fesch and, of course, that tenth muse, Madame Recamier. Even so, Canova always remained essentially Italian and was closer to Rome than Paris. Canova came by his art rather naturally, as his grandfather was a sepulchral stone cutter by profession, early marked and encouraged the boy's fondness for statuary, and saw to it that he was given an adequate art education. His greatest triumph is undoubtedly the statue of Pauline as Venus, a noble work worthy of the palmy days of Hellenic art. Through his neoclassical spectacles, the Italian artist saw Napoleon's mother as the matronly Agrippina of old, his sister Pauline, not without some justification, as Venus Victorious, and Napoleon himself, most obligingly, as a Roman emperor.

An artist who was active in France during the Directoire, Consulate and Empire, and who died at the age of 87 in 1828, was Jean-Antoine Houdon. Although he could not be said to be inferior to Canova, the fact remains that his later works never had the same complex and spontaneous elegance as those of the pre-Revolutionary period. Although he sculpted with impeccable technical perfection there seems to be a lack of soul in such works as the icy bronze *Cicero* of 1804 (*Bibliotheque Nationale*, Paris) or the *Voltaire* in the Paris Pantheon, a far cry from the magnificent portrait of the philosopher which Houdon had sculpted many years earlier, which was a masterpeice of potentially romantic Neo-Classicism with its precarious balance between nature and artifice, striking realism and abstract-idealization. A work which belongs to his least creative is the bust of the Empress Josephine executed in 1808 (Versailles), in which neither the diaphonous transparency of the marble, the exquisite modeling of each lock of hair or the glacial sumptuousness of the curves of her draperies succeed in giving life to her bloodless, pallid smile or the vacuous gravity of her splendid countenance. More expressive was the terracotta bust of Napoleon (Dijon Museum) which was his greatest achievement of the period and the only work that stands comparison with his wonderful portraits of the *Ancien Regime*. In this work there was a discreet hint of Antiquity in the studied but by no means pedantic carving of the features, ingeniously underlined by a ribbon running under the hair high above the broad forehead and flowing in cunningly calculated curves over the powerful neck. The sincerity and vehemence of the expression and its underlying impassioned firmness giving the bust an unforgetable aura of generosity and virile power. The old artist must certainly have been conscious of his success when he signed his work: '*Sa Majeste l'Empereur et Roy, fait d'apres nature, St. Cloud, Aoust 1806*'.

While not giving a description of the activities of Francois Rude (1784-1855), it should be noted that his greatest works belong to the Romantic period. Also, passing mention should be made of Denis-Antoine Chaudet (1763-1810), the author of such works as *Cupid Catching a Butterfly* (1802, Louvre), a sculpture of such sterile, glacial formalism that it might well justify the attacks made upon the Empire style by detractors incapable of seeing anything in it but an icy manifestation of an unnaturally funereal taste. A similar judgement applied to Lemot (1772-1837) and Cartellier (1757-1831), who were commissioned together with Chaudet, Moitte (1746-1810) and Roland (1746-1816) to decorate the outer wall of the Louvre. Cartellier's well-known bas-relief *Glory Distributing Wreaths* (1810) may have been appreciated by the occasional peasant, but its mechanical symmetry and insipid composition wearies the eye and recalls the uniformity of Nazi sculpture rather than the golden rules of Classical compositions. Moitte on the other hand, sometimes attained an instant of genuine aesthetic emotion, as in his *Monument of General Desaix* (1805, *Hospice du Grand St. Bernard*), in which the dying hero, gently leaning against his horse, seems to be intoning the finale of a grand opera rather than giving himself up to religious reflections. Two of these fairly successful works were produced by F. J. Bosio (1768-1845) such as the *Aristeus, God of Gardens* (1812, Louvre) which according to Janneau '*Ressortit a l' amenitie du XVIII Siecle*', and his fatuous *Henry IV* as a child of a few years later, which Louis XVIII wished to keep permanently in his study. Under the Empire it was decided to execute a scheme which the Count of Angiviller had suggested many years before: to commission a series of sculptures of great men of the past. But the work was confined to mediocre artists like Moitte and Joseph Foucou who were a far cry from sculptors such as Pajou and Clodion. The column of the *Grande Armée* in the Place Vendome offered the sculptors of the day a rare opportunity to display their talents, and Deseine, Boizot, Bosio and Bridan were some of the artists who worked on its enormous bas-reliefs. A similar though less spectacular opportunity was afforded by the Pantheon and the Arch of the Carrousel. One of the artists who worked on the Arch was Charles-Louis Corbet (1758-1808). More worthy of attention, however, is his marvelous portrait of the young Bonaparte, a work still 18th century in style but almost Romantic in spirit, with its suffusing note of sadness. It was one of the most beautiful and convincing sculptures of the dying century. Besides the gesso model in the Invalides, there is a marble version at Malmaison.

* * *

James A. Jahnke was born in Lakewood, Ohio, 1928 USMC, Retired, 1966 Non-Faculty Staff, University of Michigan Non-Faculty Staff, Seattle University. Presently employed Veterans Benefits Counselor, V.A. Medical Center, Seattle, WA. Active Member Episcopal Church. Hobbies: Operative History, Oriental Art, History and Antiqaue collector. Resides in Seattle. WA, Member NSA since 1986.

French Porcelain
by Helen Smith, Waterloo, ONT

The definition of Paris porcelain in the 18th century is simple: hard-paste porcelain both manufactured and decorated in factories situated in Paris. It becomes more complex in the 19th century when it may be defined as hard-paste porcelain, generally decorated in Paris although not invariably manufactured there, and originating either from factories with at least an official Paris address or else from salesrooms located in Paris.

The first French factory of hard-paste porcelain operated in Strassburg. It was created at the beginning of the 18th century, but used clay coming from Germany. Following the discovery of kaolin deposits in the Limousin, numerous factories were set up.

One can roughly localize the early porcelain factories to the northeast quarter of Paris. This was an artisan section where the best cabinet makers and the faience dealers were already established. Nearly every street harboured a factory, sometimes two, producing either faience or porcelain. The factories were often large quadrilateral areas around which were grouped the various buildings for producing and selling the porcelain. Sometimes housing for the manufacturer, his family and employees was included. Friendships and family ties drew the manufacturers together, with numerous marriages taking place between families.

Paris was probably favoured as a centre because of its proximity to the Court, the plentiful supply of capital and the volume of commercial activity. It also attracted numerous travellers and many such people visited the factories and bought their wares.

The most frequented factory was Guerhard and Dihl. In his diary, Governor Morris, a member of the colonial aristocracy and United States representative in Paris, noted his visits to the factory of Angoulime in 1789. He toured it with Madame de Flahaut and he bought porcelain with Washington in mind. "We find that the porcelain here is more elegant and cheaper than it is at Sevres." The next year he sent Washington a bisquite group of a woman in antique style with cupids, for which he had paid about one hundred louis.

The Parisian porcelain factories mainly worked to order. They had their models for shapes and decorations, but the customer assembled his service from whatever items he wished. He could even commission 'replacers' for Sevres, Meissen and other services, particularly if they were in common production.

Customers included courtiers and tradesmen, and in particular, the limonadiers and perfumers who were concerned with the appearence of the porcelain wares used in their business. Many professional bodies regularly bought porcelain; the goldsmiths and bronze-founders mounted vases, inlay workers set plaques and medallions into their most exquisite pieces of furniture and clock makers fitted porcelain clock cases and embellished their work with porcelain dial-plates.

The turn of the 18th century had seen a transition from Rococo to Antique simplicity. By a sort of counter-movement, the first half of the 19th century saw antique sobriety give way to prodigious luxury in both shapes and decor. Later shapes seldom regained the simplicity of the late 18th century.

However, the Oriental, especially Chinese influence was continuously in evidence. From the outset of porcelain making in Paris, many official documents such as decrees from the King's Council refer to plain, or blue-and-white Chinese porcelain. Decorations '*au Chinois*' were particularly esteemed from Louis XV's reign until the Restoration.

French hard-paste, or true porcelain, as well as soft-paste porcelain (a porcellaneous material rather than true porcelain)was made at the royal factory (now the national porcelain factory) of Sevres, near Versailles, from 1756 until the present; the industry was located earlier at Vincennes. On the decline of Meissen after 1756 from its supreme position as arbiter of fashion, Sevres became the leading porcelain factory in Europe. Perhaps the major factor contributing to its success was the patronage of Louis XV's mistress, Madame de Pompadour. It was through her influence that the move was made from Vincennes to Sevres, where she had a chateau, and through her that some of the foremost artists of the time, such as Francois Boucher and the sculptor Etienne-Maurice Falconet (who directed Sevres modelling between 1757 and 1766), became involved in the enterprise. It was after her that "rose Pompadour" was named in 1757 .This was one of many new background colours developed at Sevres, one of which, *bleu de roi* ("royal blue"; c.1757), has passed into the dictionary as a universal term.

One of the central preoccupations at Sevres, in which such notable chemists as Jean Hellot were engaged, was the secret of hard-paste porcelain. Soft paste had been made at Vincennes from 1745, but the Sevres factory did not obtain the secret of hard paste until 1761, when it was bought from Pierre-Antoine Hannong . The necessary raw materials were still lacking in France; and it was not until these were found in the Perigord district, that hard-paste porcelain could be produced. Thereafter a distinction was made in nomenclature between *porcelaine de France* or *vieuse Sevres* (soft paste, or *pate tendre*) and *porcelaine royale* (hard paste, or *pate dure*) .

Of the many styles and techniques for which Sevres became famous, some leading examples may be listed: white figures, either biscuit (unglazed) or rarely glazed, representing Boucher-like cupids, shepherdesses, or nymphs, nude, draped, or in contemporay dress, vessels decorated with flowers, exotic birds, and marine subjects. Many were embellished with patterns in gold and accentuated by fine gilding in curls, scrolls and trellis patterns. Narrative scenes from classical mythology and contemporary pastoral life were depicted. Jewelled decoration was achieved by gilt and colours being laid on like encrusted gems. Some dinner services were decorated with naturalistic birds from the famous *Natural History of Birds* (1771) of George-Louis Leclerc Buffon. Sevres went through the gamut of 18th century styles, including those associated with the reign of Louis XIV (1774-92), early 19th century under the directorship of Alexander

Brongniart. After the Neoclassical and Egyptian styles of Napoleon's empire, no one distinctive style was initiated.

Paris porcelain is indebted to England for two techniques: her coal firing which had been put into operation in the 18th century, and her transfer printing process, in common use half a century before the Parisian specialists registered their patents.

The fashion for imitations of Wedgwood ware, created by the impossibility of importing any because of the blockade, was reflected in vases, plaques and medallions. Occasionally the blue was replaced by grey or mauve.

The success of busts was derived from the taste for portraits. Prud'homme in "*L'Ancien et le Nouveau Paris*" noted that in the course of the revolution, one witnessed the appearance on mantlepieces of the busts of the latest idol. Busts of Necker, the Duc d'Orleans and LaFayette were succeeded by Mirabeau, Marat and Robespierre .

The output of biscuit ware in the 19th century was only a continuation from the preceding century, although models grew more complicated and dimensions more imposing. Services were produced entirely of biscuit adorned with reliefs, palmettes and roses, some touched with gold. A service of this type was produced by Sevres and given by Napoleon in 1813 to the Marshal Augereau.

The Cathedral style and the Egyptian influence in particular survived side by side for many years. Balzac who was reputed to have refined taste in porcelain, bought Gothic vases with black back grounds and others having Egyptian designs.

The perenniality of the Egyptian decor may be explained, not so much in terms of a reminiscence of the Egyptian Campaign, but rather as one of the side-effects of the enormous interest aroused by Champollion's deciphering of the hieroglyphics. His "*Precis du Systeme Hieroglyphique*" was published in 1824.

The Gothic style, which reached its apogee between 1820 and 1830 owed its appearance partly to the interest excited by the old monuments that Lenoir had assembled in the Paris convent called the *Couvent des Petits-Augustins*, with the object of removing them from the destructive fury of the Revolutionaries. Even for the coronation of Napoleon, the decorations in Notre-Dame were pseudoGothic. In

1811, Josephine had a Gothic gallery for her pictures constructed at Malmaison.

The repercussions of the Revolution on the porcelain trade were far-reaching. Enormous losses were inflicted by the closure of the Spanish and Russian markets. The abolition of privileges allowed complete freedom for setting up a factory and the profusion of promissory notes permitted rapid and numerous financial transactions. From this there ensued a proliferation of porcelain factories in Paris; most of them, however, unable to sustain themselves for very long. Before the Revolution there had been fifteen private factories which grew to forty-one. But by 1814 only half of them were left. Under the *"Ancien Regime"*, porcelain wares had been luxury items, intended chiefly for a wealthy clientele, whose suppression was a disasterous blow to the factories until the emergence of new customers.

The manufacture of porcelain ran into problems of manpower, and craftsmen were scarce owing to the Revolutionary wars. Transportation of raw materials was difficult and trade was stagnant everywhere. One of the most important manufacturing enterprises in the Dept. of the Seine, Dihl's porcelain factory, noted in 1801, that formerly it had employed 130 craftsmen and now had only 60.

General Lacuee, the Commander of Paris, and Frochet, the *Prefect de la Seine*, analysed the situation and recorded the discredit of promissory notes, the Terror driving away capital investment, the war hampering exports and depressing inland consumption, and the workers rising in revolt. They did record a slight resurgence of commercial activity after Brumaire 18th.

In its *Bulletin* of Thermidor 25th, Year XI (1804), the *Ministere de la Police Generale* indicated a resumption of work in porcelain factories and an increased number of craftsmen being employed. This was probably due in part to the advent of the Empire, which with its Court and pomp, produced large orders for the trade in luxuries.

The situation of the porcelain factories preoccupied the authorities, and a report from the *Bureau des Arts et Manufacture* to the Minister of the Interior in 1806 investigated ways of increasing the sale of porcelain. Whereas the manufacturers had dearly wished for freedom under the Ancien Regime, they now asked for certain limitations on the practice of work, such as the compulsory marking of wares and the control of work done by outside decorators. Before the Revolution, there had been ten factories in Paris, Sevres amongst them, out of which only four used to mark their wares.

The *Almanach du Commerce de la Ville de Paris* of 1808 enumerated in its second supplement the themes which the factories stocked. They were: Fables of La Fontaine, portraits of great men, both ancient and modern, picturesque views, castles and country houses in different lands, highlights from French and Roman history, monuments of Paris and its environs, engraved stones and military events.

In the depths of the slump, two events, quite different in character, brought about an improvement in trade; the creation of the Bank of France in 1800, which brought interest rates down, and the Treaty of Amiens in 1802 which restored some confidence. However, the former was shaken in 1805-6 when speculating merchants threatened it.

But once peace and freedom returned to the high seas, the Parisian porcelain makers started exporting their products outside Europe. In 1819 they went to the Levant to organize competition against Saxon and Austrian porcelain. Exports were not confined to the Near East. They boasted of orders from Peking, Latin America and the United States.

Strong competition appeared from Prussia in particular. After the difficult years of French occupation there, the victory over Napoleon in 1815 ushered in a brief and promising economic revival.The Royal Porcelain Manufactory,(*Konigliche Porzellan Manufaktur* (KPM)) which the French had transformed into a "*fabrique de porcelaine sous 'administration francaise*" entered a prolific period. The growth in patriotic sentiment generated by the long struggle for liberation, was mirrored in the products of the factory, and contibuted greatly to its financial success. The most important patron in the post-war years was Frederick William III who commissioned six dinner services for prominent Prussian generals who had seen service in the wars of liberation.

The preeminent military figure in the Alliance's campaign against Napoleon was Arthur Wellesley, Duke of Wellington (17691852) A large dinner service was commissioned from the KPM factory for him by the King of Prussia on Oct. 2, 1817. One of the major designers of this service was Johann Shadow, sculptor and Director of the Royal Academy of Arts This dinner service, hailed at the time as KPM's finest achievement, was pompous and redolent with hero worship and featuring rich, metallic-looking gilding, was modelled on the Napoleonic Empire style developed by Sevres in particular.

The competion faced by the Prussian factory is of interest where the Berlin dinner service is concerned, for between 1818-1820 the Duke of Wellington received three other porcelain services of note as gifts from different European monarchs. In 1818 King Louis XVIII of France presented the then British Ambassador to Paris with the *"Service Egyptien"*, a dessert service with a large architectural centrepiece, the *non plus ultra* in Egyptomania that was all the rage in France following Bonaparte's Egyptian campaign of 1799. The book on Egypt(1802) by Dominique Vivant Denon supplied the models for the monumental centre-piece, based on the Temples of Karnak, Dendera, and Philae, and for the views on the sixty-six plates. This service was originally commissioned by the Emperor Napoleon in 1811-1812 for his former wife, the Empress Josephine as a gift at the time of their divorce. She refused this gift. Some examples of this service are on display in the Wellington Museum, Apsley House, London, England, which is run by the Victoria and Albert Museum.

Despite Wellington being considered the liberator of Europe and a national hero, his popularity soon waned as a politician. Twice Apsley House was stoned by angry mobs outraged by his opposition to reform. This caused iron shutters to be fitted to the windows which may have given rise to Wellington's nick-name the "Iron Duke"

Confronted with the difficulties with which the factories were contending, Napoleon decided to grant them loans and forward orders to them. A formal command was signed by the Emperor in Ostend on March 27th, 1807, "to come to the aid of those factories of our Empire, which, through force of circumstances and lack of retail sales of merchandise manufactured by them, are suffering from shortage of funds". Some of the money for these subsidies was raised from fines imposed upon the Emperor's critics in Belgium.

In the early stages the loss of overseas outlets caused by the Continental Blockade had been offset by the growth of trade with countries invaded by the French armies. But as the Napoleonic troops fell back, the field gradually shrank and commerce found itself reduced to transactions conducted on home ground.

The conscription of 1813, the taxes, and the return to France of people who had settled in the vassal kingdoms weighed heavily upon industry and trade. Frochet encouraged Napoleon to apply controls to industry partly out of fear of rioting and violent working-class reactions. But commerce was still haunted by the spectre of war to such an extent that, on the occasion of the Spanish expedition in 1820, the manufacturers trembled.

A particularly interesting source of documentation is supplied by the industrial and commercial exhibitions held in Paris. Exhibitions of this kind mark out the economic history of France from 1789 onwards. The industrial exhibitions of the first half of the 19th century had an unquestionable influence on the emergence of the big factories. Distinctions were handed out not only on the strength of the product's quality but also the quality and price. The object was to promote exports.

In order to stimulate manufacturers of France as a whole, the first "Exhibition of the Products of French Industry", was held on the Champs-de-Mars on the last days of the Year VII(1798) Nevertheless, political events gave rise to misgivings amongst capitalists and obliterated credit.

After the *coup d'etat* of November 9, 1799, Napoleon took up residence in the Luxembourg Palace, which became the first official setting in which the new consul lived. Later he moved to the Tuileries Palace, and this became the official palace of the French government. Napoleon made the conspicuous display of luxury a matter of necessity if the French industry was to recover and thrive. He wanted to display to the foreigners returning to Paris after the peace, the wealth and resources of the State he governed. In assessing the situation he saw the need for state intervention.

Throughout his reign Napoleon was keenly interested in his palaces. He sought to create a decor that would reflect the grandeur of the power that he embodied. His interest was also stimulated by the foreign palaces discovered during his military campaigns. He sought to provide a stimulus to various craft trades, allowing them to participate in France's economic revival and to stay in business, a perennial theme of Napoleon's patronage.

Egyptology
by Arthur G. Lawson, Philadelphia, PA

It has been called a military disaster but a cultural triumph. Why did the French go to Egypt remains a controversial question. An invasion of England wasn't feasible at the time and seizing Egypt and the trade routes to India might be the next best thing. But it was risky with trouble brewing in Europe and Nelson roaming the Mediterranean. Perhaps the Directory wanted Bonaparte out of the way. As Christopher Herold put it, "It is dangerous to have unemployed heroes loitering about. "

On May 19, 1798 four hundred ships sailed from Toulon. General Bonaparte won some battles, conquered Egypt, had his fleet destroyed by Nelson and then returned to France. Less than half of the 35, 000 troops made it back.

The cultural triumph part was General Bonaparte taking 167 scientists, artists and technicians with him. They were to:

1. Study Egyptian monuments and antiquities.
2. Write a history of ancient Egypt.
3. Prepare a French-Egyptian dictionary
4. Publish two journals.

In Engineering they were to plan for a Suez Canal and a series of dams on the Nile. There were also agricultural and hospital projects as well as studying geology, astronomy, and the flora and fauna of Egypt.

To these ends the Institute of Egypt was established with the distinguished scientist, Gaspard Monge, as President and General Bonaparte as Vice President. There were four sections: 1. Math, 2.

Physics, 3. Politics and Economics, and 4. Literature and the Arts.

Republican France had dropped the 7 day week and had adopted the Egyptian decade (10 day week). Institute meetings were 2 times a decade on *Primidi* and *Sextidi* at 7 a.m, for 2 hours. Sessions were open to all general officers. Bonaparte often proposed topics and designated the debaters, e. g., Is earth the only habitable planet? How old is the earth? Is there anything in the interpretation of dreams? (As a psychologist myself, that's right up my alley. I'd say, "yes, but mostly, no. ") Other topics he proposed were focused on the practical: Can we improve the army's baking ovens? Can we brew beer without hops (hops were not present in Egypt)? Gen. Bonaparte is described as being able to talk spontaneously on almost any topic - "often banalities punctuated by flashes of intuition. "

The savants included a number of talented, fascinating individuals. Dominique Vivant Denon, an artist and a brave, dashing aristocratic Renaissance man, became the first director of the Louvre. Nicolas-Jacques Conté invented the graphite pencil. Capt. Malus discovered the principle of polarization. Geoffroy Sainte-Hilaire, a life long friend of Cuvier, conducted the first course in Zoology in Paris. Chief Surgeon was Dr. Larrey, who Napoleon later called the most virtuous man he ever met.

It wasn't easy; 34 of the 167 savants never made it back. Many had eye problems from windblown cutting sand and the blazing sun. There was the plague as well as enemy fire.

Among the papers presented at the Institute sessions were: Monge on mirages, Sucy on the need to explore the sources of the Nile, Marcel reported on Arabic poetry, and Savigny on insects and worms. Certainly the most momentous report was that of the discovery of the Rosetta Stone. However, it was more than 20 years later before Champollion cracked the code. Everyone, including Champollion, believed that hieroglyphics were strictly symbolic, the key to the deciphering was to drop that assumption. Hieroglyphics it turns out, are both symbolic and phonetic. The decipherment was too late for the Egyptian campaign's magnum opus the *Description of Egypt* which stirred so much interest in things Egyptian throughout Europe. The Rosetta Stone itself, along with some other antiquities, was seized by the victorious British army and resides today in the British Museum.

The scientists and artists studied, measured and recorded, and initiated Egyptology as a scientific study. They exploded the myth that before Homeric Greece there had only been barbarism. The loot the French were taking (which fell to the British) was modest and the emphasis was properly on scientific investigation. The British gave Egypt back to Turkish rule and Mohammed Ali, a former Albanian coffee merchant who became a Turkish general, seized power for himself by 1806. He readily sold or gave away Egyptian antiquities to curry favor with Europeans. For a time battering rams and gunpowder were used to open tombs. Although Egyptology then flourished it was not until the next century that the exodus of treasures was controlled. In 1912 the Germans managed to slip the magnificent Nefertiti bust out of the country. All of this was not of course new, we know early on the Egyptians stopped building pyramids because of tomb robbers.

* * *

Arthur Lawson is a long time NSA member and a recently retired psychologist. Winchester, Mass. is where he grew up. He's a graduate of Harvard. Napoleon the man and the myth has long fascinated him as does that period of history. In a few years the 200th anniversary of Napoleon's career will be upon us and it is not clear how this will be responded to in France and elsewhere. In this age of the politically correct, when Columbus is in trouble, the Emperor may not fare well. He thinks we ought to accept the warts. There were certainly negatives about the Egyptian campaign but there was also Napoleon at his best, leading a group of scholars, displaying his multifaceted intelligence, and personally involved in intellectual give and take.

Uniforms in the Age of Napoleon
by William B. Teefy, Castro Valley, CA

Napoleon put great store in the power of a smart looking uniform. Though he most often dressed simply and comfortably, he realized that a handsome suit of clothes lent prestige to the individual and the army as a whole. France's 25 year struggle against successive coalitions of the monarchs of Europe throughout the Revolution and Empire made the military man and his uniform the pride of his country. To be a soldier of the Emperor was to be a hero. The status of the soldier led to the creation of the many elegant and fanciful uniforms which today set the period apart from any other of the modern era. The uniforms themselves, even today, are the embodiment of glory. They so inspire the imagination with their color and panache that a hundred years after the end of the Empire the Great Powers of Europe were still dressing up and marching into machine gun fire, play acting as if the face of battle had not changed, trying to recapture that now chimerical martial splendor.

But when they were new, when these uniforms were the fashion and not merely costume, they were glorious. In the 1800's most citizens did not experience the horrors and drudgery of war. War was a bulletin, a letter, or the tales and legends of returning veterans. The uniform was the symbol of victories, of daring deeds, heroism under fire, and the camaraderie of the military order.

For the soldier, the uniform was not only the glamour of a fine outfit and prestige that came with it, but also, a part of his personal identity. It marked him as a member of a specific company, in a particular regiment; as part of a clearly defined family that ate, drank, slept and often died as a unit. His importance as an individual was related to the honor of his regiment. Part of this honor was the condition of his uniform. Every effort was made to maintain the dignity of his kit.

This was not easy in the days before consistent materials standards, mass manufactured clothing, and modern logistical support. Uniforms often were made of sub-par material, dyed improperly, or were almost unwearable due to poor workmanship. Then, as now, military contractors were sometimes more interested in the bottom line than the welfare of the troops. Even when the uniform was of reasonable quality keeping it in presentable condition during a long and arduous campaign was difficult.

On the day of battle, a soldier would try to present himself as best he could. Every effort would be made to squirrel away a good set of leggings, clean trousers, and a fresh pompon or plume for the shako or cap. The coat would be brushed as clean as possible and the brightwork shined. The reward for the regiment that could maintain appearances was quite great. The sharpest regiments would often be tagged for an imperial review, or to march in a victory parade through the next town. His appearance in the parade might not only capture the fancy of a young lady, it often meant being first in line for whatever food and lodging a town or city had to offer. The poor dredges who through negligence or bad luck were not considered presentable could find themselves camped well outside range of such comforts as a dry bed and a good tavern.

Today, it is hard to imagine the excitement of taking part in or witnessing an event like a military parade. But think of the time. The majority of the population of Europe lived a simple rural or semi-rural life. Most wore handmade clothes of rough local fabrics that were drab in color. Only the very wealthy could afford tailored clothes made of fine fabric, and only the well-to-do could spare the time and expense of travelling to a major city where there was access to the arts and fashion. A parade of well uniformed men, bursting with pride, sporting shiny buckles and bouncing plumes was an event.

Especially when proceeded by a regimental band. The bandsmen of the regiment wore the brightest and most fanciful uniforms, often of a contrasting color. Decked out in full regalia, playing a military air or popular tune, it was probably more color and sound than the average person would see throughout the rest of the year. For the soldiers, it was a bright memory to cherish, a day in the sun, a brush with fame.

Then, of course, there was the Imperial Guard. They were the elite of the elite. Caparisoned with a tall bearskin and uniformed in a finer cloth with gold epaulettes and the brightest and tallest plumes, they were the epitome of martial splendor. For the troops of the regular army, most of them peasants or laborers themselves as boys, this was tantamount to being a prince. The higher pay and extra privileges that went with membership in the guard were exemplified by their splendid apparel. This was a great motivating factor for the average soldier, something worth risking life for above and beyond the demands of duty and country.

Napoleon realized the importance of the uniform as a symbol of French power and Imperial might. The soldiers of his army became the benchmark by which other armies of his day judged their worthiness. Today, the power of those uniforms lives on in the hearts of thousands of military anachronists and hundreds of thousands of collectors, designers and artists who have an appreciation not only for the reputation of the Emperor and his army but for the beauty and style of the clothing from this rich and wonderful period, of which the uniform is the boldest expression.

• • •

William B. Teefy is a Senior Graphic Designer with SynOptics Communications, Inc. a Silicon Valley company providing computer networking solutions. He holds a B.S. degree in Graphic Design from San Jose State University. His interests are the uniforms, military history, strategy, tactics, and wargaming of the Napoleonic era. He is currently working on a history of the 3° Régiment de Hussards.

Gold and Silversmiths To Emperor Napoleon
by Robert W. Marshall, Louisville, KY

I did not have a speech format when conducting my table on the Gold and Silversmiths to Emperor Napoleon. I primarily used a letter from Armand Gelinas as the basis for my discussion and adlibbed other information I gathered. I probably gave a different talk at each twenty minute interval but some of the highlights were as follows:

According to Armand Gelinas' letter to me of September 16, 1991, Napoleon had three prominent gold and silversmiths in France. I think the most prominent one was M. G. Biennais who seems to have probably made most of the Emperor's pieces.

I found out from another source that Etienne Nitot made most of his ceremonial sabers and swords. He also made some of the marshals' batons which were quite elaborate. The Napoleon diamond which was in the handle of Napoleon's wedding sword was lost at the Battle of Waterloo when the huge carriage was captured by the British. The diamond was never heard about again. The creation of the sword was attributed to Nitot. He also made most of Napoleon's famous snuff boxes .

Claude Odiot provided many objects of art silverware. His most prominent piece was a young graceful fawn carrying a large wine cup which was molded from the breast of Pauline Borghese, the Emperor's sister. He also made many centerpieces. Another renowned piece Odiot made was a cameo diadem (crown) for Josephine which was made of gold and ceramics and was exhibited at the Metropolitan Museum of Art in March of 1990, along with another diadem set with 1,040 diamonds for the coronation which is now in the collection of

Van Cleef & Arpels and which was for sale. I don't know who bought it. It was supposedly made by Nitot.

Napoleon's Empire, though great and brilliant, did not last long enough to establish a ruling dynasty like other European countries, such as Russia, Austria and England which ran from 500 to 1,000 years. Lacking the 500 year spans, or more, to establish purveyors of jewelry, artifacts and etc. whose claim to fame would be jewelers, swordsmen or whatever to supply the Napoleonic Empire.

We also talked about many other subjects - as it was sort of a free flowing discussion.

* * *

Robert Marshall was born in Champaign, Illinois, where his father was going to school and teaching at the time. His parents were both from central Kentucky. He became interested in history in school at a very young age. Between the ages of 12 and 20 he read quite a lot about Napoleon and his decisive abilities to solve problems and accomplish great things. He has been a student of Napoleon ever since. He sometimes thinks his early studies of Napoleon and other historic figures have helped him gain a measure of success in business world.